Embracing Your Crown of Authority

Recognizing, Retrieving, and Reestablishing Your Crown of Authority

By

Dr. Ron M. Horner

Embracing Your Crown of Authority

Recognizing, Retrieving, and Reestablishing Your Crown of Authority

By

Dr. Ron M. Horner

LifeSpring International Ministries
PO Box 5847
Pinehurst, North Carolina 28374
www.RonHorner.com

Embracing Your Crown of Authority

Recognizing, Retrieving, and Reestablishing Your Crown of Authority

Copyright © 2025 Dr. Ron M. Horner

All rights reserved. This book is protected by the copyright laws of the United States of America. It may not be copied or reprinted for commercial gain or profit. The use of short quotations or occasional page copying for personal, or group study is permitted and encouraged. Permission will be granted upon request.

Trademarks used are the property of their respective owners.

Scripture is taken from the New King James Version®. Copyright © 1982 by Thomas Nelson. Used by permission. All rights reserved. (Unless otherwise noted.)

Scripture quotations marked (KJV) are taken from the KING JAMES VERSION, public domain.

Scripture quotations marked (NASB) are taken from the NEW AMERICAN STANDARD BIBLE®, Copyright© 1960, 1962, 1963, 1968, 1971, 1972, 1973, 1975, 1977, 1995 by The Lockman Foundation. Used by permission.

Scripture quotations marked (NIV) are taken from THE HOLY BIBLE, NEW INTERNATIONAL VERSION®. Copyright© 1973, 1978, 1984, 2011 by Biblica, Inc.™. Used by permission of Zondervan.

Scripture quotations marked (NLT) are taken from the Holy Bible, New Living Translation, copyright ©1996, 2004, 2015 by Tyndale House Foundation. Used by permission of

Tyndale House Publishers, Carol Stream, Illinois 60188. All rights reserved.

Scripture quotations marked (THE MIRROR) is taken from The Mirror Study Bible by Francois du Toit. Copyright © 2021 All Rights Reserved. Used by permission of the author.

Scripture quotations marked (TPT) is taken from The Passion Translation®. Copyright ©2017, 2018 by Passion and Fire Ministries, Inc. Used by permission. All rights reserved. ThePassionTranslation.com.

Requests for bulk sales discounts, editorial permissions, or other information should be addressed to:

LifeSpring Publishing
PO Box 5847
Pinehurst, NC 28374 USA

Additional copies available at RonHorner.com

ISBN 13 TP: 978-1-953684-65-3
ISBN 13 eBook: 978-1-953684-66-0

Cover Design by Darian Horner Design
(www.darianhorner.com)
Image: 123rf.com #85093814

First Edition: June 2025

10 9 8 7 6 5 4 3 2 1 0

Printed in the United States of America

Table of Contents

Acknowledgments i
Characters in this Book iii
Preface v
Chapter 1 The Court of Crowns 1
Chapter 2 The Crown of a Revelation Receiver 11
Chapter 3 The Books of Crowns 15
Chapter 4 The Crown of Crowns 47
Chapter 5 Your Crown of Authority 53
Chapter 6 The Crown of Sonship 69
Chapter 7 The Crown of Everlasting 79
Chapter 8 Discovering the Crown of Discernment 85
Chapter 9 Types of Crowns in Scripture Part 1 89
Chapter 10 Types of Crowns in Scripture Part 2 111
Chapter 11 Types of Crowns in Scripture Part 3 127
Chapter 12 Undesirable Crowns 137
Chapter 13 Crowns Not Listed in Scripture 155
Chapter 14 Crown of Wisdom 159

Chapter 15 The Royal Priesthood of the Crown........ 167

Chapter 16 Crown of Bené Elohim 173

Chapter 17 The Superior Crown 185

Chapter 18 Crown of the Bride 197

Chapter 19 Crowns of Conquest 205

Chapter 20 Crown of Creativity 215

Chapter 21 Crowns in a Storm 223

Chapter 22 Every Crown Has a Mantle 229

Chapter 23 The Superior Crown of Glory 239

Chapter 24 The Superior Crown of Starlight 245

Chapter 25 The Crown of Immortality 249

Chapter 26 Crowns & Technologies 253

Chapter 27 The Crown of Kingdom Expansion 259

Chapter 28 The False Crown of Deception
or Crown of Deceit (The First Crown) 267

Chapter 29 The False Crown of Loathing
(The Third Crown) 285

Chapter 30 The False Crown of Fear
(The Second Crown) 297

Chapter 31 The False Crown of Devouring
(The Seventh Crown) 307

Chapter 32 The False Crown of Magic
(The Fifth Crown) 319

Chapter 33 The False Crown of Secrets
(The Sixth Crown) 331

Chapter 34 The False Crown of Antichrist
(The Fourth Crown) 341

Chapter 35 Prayer of Freedom
from the Seven False Crowns 357

Chapter 36 Crown of Righteousness 361

Chapter 37 Retrieving Lost Crowns 367

Appendix 371

   Learning to Live Spirit First 373

   Resources from LifeSpring 381

   Works Cited 387

   Description 389

   About the Author 391

   Other Books by Dr. Ron M. Horner 393

Acknowledgments

Thanks go to Ian Clayton for teaching on the subject of crowns in 2016. It was from that teaching that Stephanie, my seer, and I were open to the contents of this book. She did a fabulous job of helping me engage with Heaven for revelation on this topic. Thanks also go to my lovely wife, Adina, with whom I shared aspects of this book and received feedback.

———— ∞ ————

Characters in this Book

In this book, we introduce you to several entities who assisted us in its writing:

Adina – Ron Horner's wife, a psalmist and minstrel.

Alicia – our Heavenly Resources Manager (what we might refer to as our HR person).

Einstein – the physicist, is a man in white that we have encountered often.

Ezekiel – the chief angel over LifeSpring International Ministries.

Gloria – a woman in white who serves as our chief legal counsel.

John – the Apostle, writer of The Revelation

Lydia – a woman in white who assists LifeSpring.

Malcolm – a man in white who often tutors us. He is also the Headmaster of CourtsNet.

Mary – the mother of Jesus.

Mary Magdalene – One of Jesus' disciples.

Moses – the Old Testament patriarch who led the children of Israel out of Egypt and towards their promised land.

Stephanie – the chief operating officer of LifeSpring International Ministries and a prolific seer.

Wisdom – the entity Wisdom spoken of in Proverbs, sometimes referred to as Lady Wisdom.

───── ∞ ─────

Preface

In early 2025, we found ourselves teaching about crowns. As a young boy growing up in church, I recall hearing some sermons about crowns that were always related to something you might receive when you got to Heaven, but I never studied it after that. It seemed to be a reward system for good behavior. Little did I know that Heaven viewed it far differently than I did. Crowns are not so much for our future in Heaven because we need them now.

Crowns are for now!

Also, I am writing this to those who know their position as sons of God. It is not a gender-based designation but rather a positionally-based one. Sons want to pursue a relationship with the Father that may be outside the norm. They are open to the idea that the Father still speaks to people today and that not all we needed to know was included in the 66 books we call our Bible. The Father has more to say. Sons—I am speaking to *you*.

Crowns Represent Dominions

When we understand that crowns represent dominions or areas of dominion, we can begin to fathom the importance of obtaining crowns, regaining lost, stolen, or forfeited crowns, and maintaining our crowns. You may have had an area where you conquered and received a crown related to that victory; however, somewhere along the way, you lost that crown, whether by your own actions or by the actions of others. You may have had a time in your life when your zeal for the Father was much stronger than it is currently. Did something happen to cause that zeal to wane? Chances are someone stole the Crown of Zeal from you, or you surrendered it. When you did, the strength and anointing accompanying that crown also lifted from your life. Do you remember the joy and energy you had before losing that crown? Don't you want it back?

Satan does not want you to have or maintain the dominion that the crown represents, so he will try to orchestrate a capturing of that crown from your life. If he is successful, he will then have removed your authority in that area of your life where you once had victory and strength. If you have an area of your life where you once had strength and no longer possess that strength, that indicates that you lost that crown in some fashion. We will talk more about this later.

Revelation 3:11:

> *Do not let tough times make me seem distant from you. I am at hand—see my nearness, not my absence. And* ***don't let temporal setbacks diminish your own authority, either.*** *Remember that you call the shots; you wear the crown.* ***My crown endorses your crown.*** *(Lit. Let nothing take your crown. Revelation 1:5; He is the King of kings and Lord of lords. Not King of slaves. Revelation 19:16. See Psalm 103:4 He redeems his life from the Pit and weaves a crown for him out of loving-kindness and tender mercies.) (MIRROR) (Emphasis mine)*

Ways You Can Lose a Crown

In this Preface, I will list different ways you can lose a crown. I won't explain much here since, throughout this book, you will read about engagements supporting what we have discovered.

- **Embracing unbelief:** If you have had a belief (in line with scripture) and you had a change of heart about that issue, the crown associated with that belief can be lost.

- **Theft:** Some (humans or others) will come into your life with the intent of stealing your crown(s).
- **Bitterness:** We can embrace offense in such a manner that we forfeit the crowns that we have received.
- **The words of others:** Other people's words can impact us in such a way that we essentially surrender our crown(s) to those words.
- **Direct action of Satan:** Satan is always roaming about, seeking those whose crowns he can steal. Don't be a victim.
- **By casting our pearls before swine:** Wisdom has to be gained, and often, we are not discerning and allow our wisdom to be distributed to those who have chosen to wallow in mud and not embrace the promises of God.
- **Disobedience:** Queen Vashti is a prime example of disobedience resulting in the loss of a crown. The story is covered in depth later in the book.
- **Trauma:** One of the purposes of trauma is to cause us to lose our crowns. The more severe the trauma, the more likely the loss of crowns (and not typically just one crown, but often several of them).
- **Foxes:** Those who work with Satan to steal crowns from the sons. (Lamentations 5:18)
- **Unchecked Pride:** "Pride goes before destruction, And a haughty spirit before a fall." (Proverbs 16:18)

- Other means not listed here may show up later in this book.

The writer of Lamentations speaks of the loss of a crown in Lamentations 5:16-22:

> [16] **The crown has fallen from our head.** Woe to us, for <u>we have sinned!</u>
>
> [17] Because of this our heart is faint; because of these things, our eyes grow dim;
>
> [18] Because of Mount Zion, which is desolate, with **foxes** walking about on it.

Petition for Restoration:

> [19] You, O LORD, remain forever; your throne from generation to generation.
>
> [20] Why do You forget us forever and forsake us for so long a time?
>
> [21] Turn us back to You, O LORD, and we will be restored; renew our days as of old,
>
> [22] Unless You have utterly rejected us and are very angry with us! (Emphasis mine)

Your crown can fall from your head because of sin.

Look again at verse 18:

*[18]{.sup} Because of Mount Zion, which is desolate, with **foxes walking about on it**. (Emphasis mine)*

These foxes were intent on stealing crowns.

With the loss of a crown:

- Your heart becomes faint. The strength you once carried in that arena is no longer present.
- Your eyes grow dim (it can affect your spiritual sight or perception).
- You become susceptible to those who would pillage your belongings, plague your life, and steal your crowns—foxes. Foxes can be spiritual beings as well as people. (Song of Solomon 2:15; Luke 13:32)

In Song of Solomon 2:15, we are instructed to catch the foxes that would spoil the vines. These foxes seek to steal the crown from your head—the anointing and authority you carry that you are to produce change in the Earth with. Tender grapes are not quite ready for harvest and need protection from those who would impact their life by premature destruction. From the crushing of grapes comes sweet wine.

Song of Solomon 2:15:

Catch us the foxes, The little foxes that spoil the vines, for our vines have tender grapes.

This is not an exhaustive list, but as we move forward and realize that we have lost, forfeited, or had crowns stolen in many ways, we want to learn how to get our crowns back and the authority that goes with them. You will learn about the Court of Crowns, the Crown of Sonship, Superior Crowns vs. inferior crowns, and many other crowns, including the false crowns of the red dragon in Revelation. This book will also teach you how to retrieve lost crowns and so much more.

Get Ready

Pause and position your soul in its seat of rest, call your spirit forward, and begin to read from within the realms of Heaven to maximize the information you are receiving.

At times, you may need to pause and enlarge your soul and request the oil of ease to be applied to your soul because, as you read, your soul may want to come forward and ask many questions. Get the input first and understand that the answers will come. Maybe not today or tomorrow, but they will come as you learn to rest in the Father's presence.

We also understand that as we engage with Heaven, we may be assisted by angels, men or women in white linen, or others from the realms of Heaven. They have much they can teach us, and as we move forward in our pursuit of revelation to assist the growth of the sons, we avail ourselves of what they have to say. We invite you to do the same.

From Chapter 27 onward, the revelations are included in the order they were received, with one exception. Therefore, some understandings may be clarified in a later chapter as more revelation is given.

Enjoy!

———— ∞ ————

Chapter 1

The Court of Crowns

As a ministry, each Tuesday evening at 7:00 PM (Eastern), we hold what is known as our LifeSpring Mentoring Group via Zoom, where we share testimonies, teachings, and recent revelations with our audience. At a recent weekly session, we taught about retrieving lost crowns. This subject was taught by Ian Clayton in 2016 and it came to my attention recently. I felt impressed by Holy Spirit to teach along those same lines in that session. It was quite fruitful. The following day, when engaging with Heaven, I heard:

> *The restoration of crowns is just the beginning. Many have lost territories that need to be restored. Others have lost inheritances that need restoration. Now that they have gone in and reclaimed their crowns, have them step into the Court of Crowns and receive renewed authorization for the authority that had been lost. It is part of the retaking of lands and*

properties, gold, and treasure, all of which have been waiting for the sons to step into a new level of sonship in this day and hour. That which has been stolen needs to be reclaimed, and that is done sevenfold.

Later that morning, Stephanie, my seer, and I determined to learn more about crowns. We asked to step into Heaven and requested entrance into the Court of Crowns, and as we came to the double doors at the court's entry, we saw that they were made of beautiful wood. The doors were closed but had intricate carvings of a giant crown on the face of the door. It reminded us of the wood King Solomon used to build the temple. As we entered, we could see it was not a typical courtroom with a judge's bench, but it was as if we were inside a giant tree. We saw indentions in the walls of the tree, and crowns seemed to be everywhere.

We asked for someone to provide counsel and Lydia, our Chief Business Advisor, came forth wearing what appeared to be a veil, but more like a train for a wedding dress. On the train, there were many crowns. We could see that there were crowns everywhere on one wall of the court, yet on the other wall, we saw empty shelves. We learned that the empty shelves were because sons had been receiving their crowns and had yet to be replenished.

The side filled with crowns contained crowns to be given to the sons. She said that the blank spaces on the wall provide those in Heaven with much joy, for the sons are coming into their own and receiving their crowns. The side with the crowns contained crowns that were still to be released.

We were walking through a vast area. It reminded us of being inside a cave, but it was a tree. We asked if this was the Tree of Life. Lydia replied that it was "something like that." As we continued to walk, the floor turned gold. The cobblestones were golden, and they were alive.

She asked, "Did you know that living stones are what are placed on many grounds?"

You are living stones, and living stones are continually added to you.

As we continued walking, we went past the gold and stepped through what seemed to be a tunnel with grass everywhere. We could smell water. We came to what appeared to be a massive canyon. We could not go any further; we could only look around.

"Why have we stopped, Lydia? What would you have us learn right here?" we asked.

She answered, "Look down."

Stephanie described what she was seeing: "It goes down forever."

"Look to my east and my west," Lydia spoke.

Stephanie responded, "Well, I feel like to my left I can see the end, but to my right, it goes on forever, and as I look up, I realize what I thought was a ceiling is actually water above us. Where are we?"

Lydia said something curious; "This is your capacity."

"What does that mean?" we asked.

Stephanie added, "At first, I thought you were saying 'capacity' like this is all I can understand, but you're not. You are saying this is mine. This is my capacity for what I have and hold. It is vast, and it is deep. This is the capacity to be filled."

"How do we fill it? It seems filled with lost treasure, lost territory, lost time, and lost peace, but the capacity is great. What do we do?" Stephanie inquired.

Lydia replied, "The severity of the loss to the sons has been great, but the measure with which they will be given is greater."

Stephanie said, "I'm beginning to see all the crowns that are on my head. I feel like I'm supposed to cast my crowns, but I don't understand. Am I supposed to cast my crowns here supernaturally?[1] What does that mean?"

---

[1] Revelation 4:9-11 ⁹ Whenever the living creatures give glory and honor and thanks to Him who sits on the throne, who lives

Lydia responded, "If this is your capacity, then casting your crowns is not taking them away from you, it's adding it to you. Just try it."

"Okay, so I cast my Crown of Endurance," Stephanie spoke. "When I did that, it lit up?"

Lydia queried, "Is your crown *not* your authority?"

Your crown is your authority.

"Yes," Stephanie answered.

"Then use your authority to call in the treasure," Lydia instructed.

---

*Use your authority
to call in the treasure*

Stephanie immediately responded,

As a son, we call in the treasure that has been lost from the north, the south, the east, and the west in every age, realm, dimension, and time to fill the capacity of this section.

---

forever and ever, [10] the twenty-four elders fall down before Him who sits on the throne and worship Him who lives forever and ever, and cast their crowns before the throne, saying: [11] "You are worthy, O Lord, to receive glory and honor and power; for You created all things, and by Your will they exist and were created."

She noted, "I saw, as I threw it out, it was just a section of the capacity. I see, from this Crown of Endurance, waterfalls beginning to form. It's as if we are creating in this capacity in this place, which is like a blank slate to fill it.

"We claim the land, properties, houses, and commercial properties that have been lost. We call them back to us. We claim that here as we cast this crown.

"I don't want this to be complicated," Stephanie added.

Lydia countered, "Well then, don't complicate it."

Stephanie replied,

In the authority that we have, we cast all of our crowns out into the space that from the north, south, east, and the west, we, as governing sons, make a proclamation and a statement that all that has been stolen from us, from every Crown of Authority, we stand and govern from because of Jesus. We make a demand in the spirit for those things to be brought back sevenfold,[2] to fill up the capacity that is here for us to hold, that has been given to us as sons in the name of Jesus—every room to be filled, every indention, every depth and every height.[3]

---

[2] Proverbs 6:31

[3] See Ephesians 3:14-21

Lydia reminded us of 1 Corinthians 2:9-10:

> *⁹ But as it is written: 'Eye has not seen, nor ear heard, nor have entered into the heart of man the things which God has prepared for those who love him.' ¹⁰ But God has revealed them to us through His Spirit. For the Spirit searches all things, yes, the deep things of God.*

---
*This is life
and that more abundantly.*

We then found ourselves in a courtroom and Stephanie began:

Lord, we present to you the books of our generations. The books of all of the prayers and supplications that have gone forth and now the crowns that have been reestablished and the capacity with which you are showing us to present to you.

We call forth the restoration of my generations. In every place that we have had crowns and resources, territories, inheritances, finances, children, peace, houses, vineyards, gifts and callings lost, stolen or forfeited, we ask that they be re-established. We ask that they be put on record and put in our books to fill the capacity to the brim more than we could think or imagine. We ask for a release from the north, south, east, and west.

We commission the angels to go to those reservoirs, those hiding places where things were stolen and taken and to bring them back in their fullness. For we, as governing sons, take the riches of Heaven, the riches in the Earth that have been given to us.

We are thankful for this court, for the knowledge and understanding, and for the capacity that you've given us. May God be glorified.

Lydia began to instruct us:

1. **The first step is to go to the Court of Crowns and receive renewed authorization for the authority that had been lost.** Simply request this authorization of the court, having done repentance for losing that crown.
2. **Then, commission the angels to begin bringing in what has been lost and fill the capacity**, which can also be enlarged.

Stephanie prayed,

Where we laid down our authority, or our generations did, and stepped out of our authority, we want to acknowledge that and take responsibility for it. We repent of it and ask that the authority and territory that had been taken be re-established in the name of Jesus.

We ask of this court for a renewed authorization of the authority that had been lost due to the forfeiture of our crown(s).

We also thank the court for the establishment and the capacity of the promised land that have not been able to come forth because of us not governing correctly as sons, but we now understand the capacity of what we are and whose we are as we indeed take in the territory, the lands, the inheritances, and all that has been established here in the name of Jesus. We commission the angels to bring these things from this place into the natural on behalf of the sons for us to be good stewards of what you give us.

As Stephanie prayed, she got a bird's eye view of the Court of Crowns and realized we were inside a crown.

Retrieving Lost Crowns

1. **Repent** for any part we held in the loss of our crown(s).
2. **Access the Court of Crowns and request renewed authorization** for the authority that had been lost. Simply request this authorization of the court, having done repentance for losing that crown.
3. **Commission the angels** to begin bringing in what has been lost and fill the capacity that you carry, which can also be enlarged.

———— ∞ ————

Chapter 2

The Crown

of a Revelation Receiver

Stephanie shared my desire to understand what we were learning and how to apply it easily. We asked, "Is there a crown related to that?"

Lydia responded, "I thought you would never ask. And yes, we are inside of a crown."

Following an unction, Stephanie said,

I'm asking, for and on behalf of ourselves and others, the Crown of a Revelation Receiver. We receive it as the Lord has made us worthy.

Stephanie realized that the Spirit of Revelation was the one bringing this crown. She added:

We acknowledge and honor the Spirit of Revelation and, as these crowns come upon our heads, for it to be guarded.

She heard many voices in unison, "Mind your mouth."

The Court of Crowns is for the sons.

We have an open invitation. This is where many will come to learn and be re-established into the territories and the promised land they have been shown.

Stephanie prayed:

Help us to mind our mouths so we do not lose the very crowns that are being established with us today, as well as the territories and those things that have been stolen.

Heaven wants us to know something significant about capacity. It's not the capacity to understand. It is the capacity of what is ours, the expansion of it, and how to fill this capacity.

1 Corinthians 2:9:

> But as it is written: 'Eye has not seen, nor ear heard, nor have entered into the heart of man the things which **God has prepared for those who love Him.**'

We are established in our walk
with the Father based on
the revelations that are revealed.

Romans 16:25:

*Now to Him who is able to **establish** you according to my gospel and the preaching of Jesus Christ, **according to the revelation of the mystery** kept secret since the world began. (Emphasis mine)*

The purpose of revelation is to establish you as sons.

The enemy of revelation is religion.

It has the following characteristics:

- Religion will always look upon revelation with disdain.
- Religion will always seek to limit or control the flow and content of revelation.
- Religion will always seek to keep revelation subservient to the wisdom of men.
- Religion will always seek to limit the application of revelation in one's life.
- Religion always makes it hard to know the Father.

———— ∞ ————

Chapter 3

The Books of Crowns

A few days later, during our engagement with Heaven, we had specifically stepped into the Library of Revelation to learn more about crowns. We saw three books on the subject, and Stephanie pulled them off the shelf. The first book's cover looked like the entrance to the Court of Crowns we had seen a few days before. The second book had no image on the cover, while the third had a rich, purple-colored cover, reminding us of royalty.

We sat down at a table in the library and we asked which book we were to look at first. We also asked for someone to come and tutor us.

Mary, the mother of Jesus, came in. Stephanie was shocked, as she was not expecting Mary. She was very young and beautiful. Stephanie suddenly understood that Mary was present because she had carried the King of kings inside herself when she was pregnant with Jesus.

Stephanie began, "It's my honor to meet you, Mary."

Mary replied, "I'll tell you what the angels said to me, 'Do not be afraid.'"

Mary began to teach us, saying there was a vast amount of intellect and information around the crowns and the authority they bring regarding the sons' positional, spiritual, and intellectual positions. We would learn from these three volumes.

Stephanie responded, "I'm eager to learn, Mary, and I will not be afraid."

Mary continued, "There are characteristics of crowns that each of us carry. It is a type of mantle in many respects.

Just as mantles represent anointings, so do crowns.

Crowns carry the Glory.

"Many have had their crowns usurped[4] without even realizing it."

She asked, "Have you searched the crowns in Revelation?"

"Yes," I replied.

She said, "That's where we will begin. As you know, Jesus does not come as a lamb but as a lion in His return.

"The New Jerusalem is set inside of a crown. Why do you think they describe the walls the way they do? From a bird's-eye view, you will see a crown and every jewel."

Revelation 21:1-27:

> *[1] Now I saw a new heaven and a new earth, for the first heaven and the first earth had passed away. Also, there was no more sea.*
>
> *[2] Then I, John, saw the holy city, New Jerusalem, coming down out of heaven from God, prepared as a bride adorned for her husband. [3] And I heard a loud voice from heaven saying, 'Behold, the tabernacle of God is with men, and He will dwell with them, and they shall be His people. God Himself will be with them and be their God. [4] And God will wipe away every tear from their*

---

[4] Usurp – to take a position of power by force or illegally.

eyes; there shall be no more death, nor sorrow, nor crying. There shall be no more pain, for the former things have passed away.'

⁵ Then He who sat on the throne said, 'Behold, I make all things new.' And He said to me, 'Write, for these words are true and faithful.' ⁶ And He said to me, 'It is done! I am the Alpha and the Omega, the Beginning and the End. I will give of the fountain of the water of life freely to him who thirsts. ⁷ He who overcomes shall inherit all things, and I will be his God, and he shall be My son. ⁸ But the cowardly, unbelieving, abominable, murderers, sexually immoral, sorcerers, idolaters, and all liars shall have their part in the lake which burns with fire and brimstone, which is the second death.'

⁹ Then one of the seven angels who had the seven bowls filled with the seven last plagues came to me and talked with me, saying, 'Come, I will show you the bride, the Lamb's wife.' ¹⁰ And he carried me away in the Spirit to a great and high mountain, and showed me the great city, the holy Jerusalem, descending out of heaven from God, ¹¹ having the glory of God. Her light was like a most precious stone, like a jasper stone, clear as crystal. ¹² Also she had a great and high wall with twelve gates, and twelve angels at the gates, and names written on them, which are the names of the twelve tribes of the children of

Israel: ^{13} *three gates on the east, three gates on the north, three gates on the south, and three gates on the west.*

^{14} *Now the wall of the city had twelve foundations, and on them were the names of the twelve apostles of the Lamb.* ^{15} *And he who talked with me had a gold reed to measure the city, its gates, and its wall.* ^{16} *The city is laid out as a square; its length is as great as its breadth. And he measured the city with the reed: twelve thousand furlongs. Its length, breadth, and height are equal.*

^{17} *Then he measured its wall: one hundred and forty-four cubits, according to the measure of a man, that is, of an angel.* ^{18} *The construction of its wall was of jasper, and the city was pure gold, like clear glass.*

^{19} *The foundations of the wall of the city were adorned with all kinds of precious stones: the first foundation was jasper, the second sapphire, the third chalcedony, the fourth emerald,* ^{20} *the fifth sardonyx, the sixth sardius, the seventh chrysolite, the eighth beryl, the ninth topaz, the tenth chrysoprase, the eleventh jacinth, and the twelfth amethyst.*

^{21} *The twelve gates were twelve pearls: each individual gate was of one pearl. And the street of the city was pure gold, like transparent glass.*

²² But I saw no temple in it, for the Lord God Almighty and the Lamb are its temple.

*²³ The city had no need of the sun or of the moon to shine in it, for the glory of God illuminated it. The Lamb is its light. ²⁴ And the nations of those who are saved shall walk in its light, and **the kings of the earth bring their glory and honor into it.***

²⁵ Its gates shall not be shut at all by day (there shall be no night there). ²⁶ And they shall bring the glory and the honor of the nations into it. ²⁷ But there shall by no means enter it anything that defiles, or causes an abomination or a lie, but only those who are written in the Lamb's Book of Life. (Emphasis mine)

Every placement is a picture of part of the crown. That crown is the picture of the atonement, the security it provides, and the placement of sons.

As sons, you will live, move, and have your being in and from that crown.

There is a revelation in and through (the book of) Revelation beyond the scope of crowns, but in all the authority He has given to the sons through the atonement of the crown.

Likewise, **you have each been given crowns—a representation of who He is to you.** It is indeed seen in the spirit, and in this space, you are a threat to the enemy, which is why he seeks whom he should devour.

---
*Those sons who do not know
their identity are at great risk.*

The lack of identity is due to a lack of one's crown.

Crowns bring identity!

---

*The theft of a crown
is what Satan seeks.*

To de-crown you is to dethrone you.

---

*To dethrone you is to minimize your
placement and your destiny.*

Your authority is then given to another.

Understanding your loss of crowns has been the first step. Retrieving them is the next step, but understanding the authority of the crowns is true revelation.

Understanding the authority of the crowns is true revelation.

At this point, Mary asked Stephanie to open the first book she had seen with the image of the double doors.

Stephanie remarked, "Do you know what I am seeing? I saw an actual movie after I opened the doors of when Satan fell.[5] **The first thing that was removed from him was his crown before he was thrown out of Heaven, and that's why he seeks ours.** Not only does he **steal our crowns**, but *he then wears them* because *it has given him authority over us and our situations in those moments.* **The loss that you feel in your being when your crowns are removed is the perpetual state in which he exists.**"

The removal of his crown has caused him to lust after the sons and the authority of the crowns that they wear.

---

[5] Luke 10:18 And He (Jesus) said to them, "I saw Satan fall like lightning from Heaven."

The crowns that we have lost or forfeited represent the authority we have also lost.

Crowns are a vitally important part of our walk.

---

*The more crowns you remove
from Satan's kingdom
and take back as sons,
the less authority
and roaming he will have.*

In 1 Peter 5, we read how the enemy seeks those who He may devour (v. 8). See 1 Peter 5:1-11. We have always been taught that he was simply seeking to destroy us through sin and temptation. However, the context is that he is seeking to de-crown us so he can de-throne us.

---

*Satan seeks to de-crown us
so he can de-throne us.*

---

1 Peter 5:1-11:

¹ The elders who are among you I exhort, I who am a fellow elder and a witness of the sufferings of Christ, and also a partaker of the glory that will be revealed:

² Shepherd the flock of God which is among you, serving as overseers, not by compulsion but willingly, not for dishonest gain but eagerly;

*³ nor as being lords over those entrusted to you, but being examples to the flock; ⁴ and when the Chief Shepherd appears, you will **receive the Crown of Glory** that does not fade away.*

⁵ Likewise, you younger people, submit yourselves to your elders. Yes, all of you be submissive to one another and be clothed with humility, for 'God resists the proud, but gives grace to the humble.'

⁶ Therefore humble yourselves under the mighty hand of God, that He may exalt you in due time, ⁷ casting all your care upon Him, for He cares for you.

*⁸ Be sober, be vigilant; because your adversary, the devil, walks about like a roaring lion, **seeking whom he may devour** [seeking whose crown he can steal]. ⁹ Resist him, steadfast in the faith, [with your crown firmly seated on your head] knowing that the same sufferings are experienced by your brotherhood in the world. ¹⁰ But may the God of all grace, who called us to His eternal glory by Christ Jesus, after you have suffered a while, perfect, establish, strengthen, and settle you.*

*¹¹ To Him be the glory and the **dominion** forever and ever. Amen. (Emphasis mine)*

> *Crowns are an expression of dominion.*

Peter gives clues on how to protect and safeguard our crowns. To the younger ones: (1) stay submitted to your elders, (2) walk in submission, and (3) walk in humility because that will result in grace being given to maintain your crown.

> *Unchecked pride can result in the loss of your crown.*

Peter recommends that we **be sober** and **vigilant** because our enemy—the accuser—is walking about seeking whom he may devour or dethrone. We are told to resist him with unmovable faith. We can recognize that others are experiencing the same things we are. However, we have hope that, as we endure, he will perfect us, establish us (in greater levels of authority), strengthen us, and settle us. In verse 11, he points out that the ultimate dominion is His.

> *Lucifer lost his crown when he rebelled and was cast out of Heaven.*
>
> *That is why he lusts after the crowns of the sons.*

> *Once he obtains a crown from a son,*
> *he wears it to confiscate*
> *the dominion it represents.*

In Amos, we read another passage about an adversary roaming:

> *Therefore, thus says the Lord GOD: 'An adversary shall be **all around the land**; He shall sap your strength from you, And your **palaces shall be plundered.**' (Amos 3:11) (Emphasis mine)*

A palace is where one lives who has a crown and the adversary wants to steal crowns.

> He wants to steal YOUR crown.

In an upcoming chapter on the False Crown of Devouring, you will learn more about the purposes of the enemy in his roaming the Earth.

The Story of Job

Satan was jealous of Job and the crowns he possessed. Job lived godly and was a trophy of God's goodness in the land of Uz. Satan wanted the crowns Job possessed for his own ends. His attempts were ultimately futile. We can learn some lessons from Job, however.

Round 1

Job 1:1-22:

> *¹ There was a man in the land of Uz, whose name was Job; and that man was blameless and upright, and one who feared God and shunned evil. ² And seven sons and three daughters were born to him. ³ Also, his possessions were seven thousand sheep, three thousand camels, five hundred yoke of oxen, five hundred female donkeys, and a very large household, so that this man was the greatest of all the people of the East.*

His wealth was a demonstration of the crowns he wore. He had a Crown of Provision, a Crown of Abundance, and a Crown of Stewardship. Satan wanted them all.

> *⁴ And his sons would go and feast in their houses, each on his appointed day, and would send and invite their three sisters to eat and drink with them.*

Job also possessed a Family Crown and a Crown of Intercession which Satan wanted.

⁵ So it was when the days of feasting had run their course, that Job would send and sanctify them, and he would rise early in the morning and offer burnt offerings according to the number of them all. For Job said, 'It may be that my sons have sinned and cursed God in their hearts.' Thus, Job did regularly.

Part of maintaining his Family Crown involved regular intercession on behalf of his children. Thus, he had a Crown of Intercession. In Job 42, he uses the Crown of Intercession to pray for his friends.

⁶ Now there was a day when **the sons of God** *came to present themselves before the LORD, and Satan also came among them. ⁷ And the LORD said to Satan,* <u>*'From where do you come?'*</u> *So Satan answered the LORD and said,* ***'From going to and fro on the earth, and from walking back and forth on it.'***

Satan's surveillance involved looking for crowns.

⁸ Then the LORD said to Satan, 'Have you considered My servant Job, that there is none like him on the earth, a blameless and upright man, one who fears God and shuns evil?'

⁹ So Satan answered the LORD and said, 'Does Job fear God for nothing?

¹⁰ Have You not made a hedge around him, around his household, and around all that he has on every side? You have blessed the work of his hands, and his possessions have increased in the land. ¹¹ But now, stretch out Your hand and touch all that he has, and he will surely curse You to Your face!'

Satan made accusations against God and Job. Job had built the hedge by his good deeds and the intercession for his children. Satan noted that God had blessed the work of Job's hands and that he had experienced increase. Satan was wrong in his final point that Job would curse God. He didn't understand the closeness of the relationship between God and Job.

¹² And the LORD said to Satan, 'Behold, all that he has is in your power; only do not lay a hand on his person.' So Satan went out from the presence of the LORD.

God granted permission to Satan to mess with Job.

¹³ Now there was a day when his sons and daughters were eating and drinking wine in their oldest brother's house; ¹⁴ and a messenger came to Job and said, 'The oxen were plowing and the donkeys feeding beside them, ¹⁵ when the Sabeans raided them and took them away—indeed they have killed the servants with the edge of the sword, and I alone have escaped to tell you!'

¹⁶ While he was still speaking, another also came and said, 'The fire of God fell from heaven and burned up the sheep and the servants and consumed them, and I alone have escaped to tell you!'

¹⁷ While he was still speaking, another also came and said, 'The Chaldeans formed three bands, raided the camels and took them away, yes, and killed the servants with the edge of the sword, and I alone have escaped to tell you!'

¹⁸ While he was still speaking, another also came and said, 'Your sons and daughters were eating and drinking wine in their oldest brother's house, ¹⁹ and suddenly a great wind came from across the wilderness and struck the four corners of the house, and it fell on the young people, and they are dead, and I alone have escaped to tell you!'

*²⁰ Then **Job arose, tore his robe,** and **shaved his head;** and he **fell to the ground** and **worshiped**. ²¹ And he said: 'Naked I came from my mother's womb, And naked shall I return there. The LORD gave, and the LORD has taken away; Blessed be the name of the LORD.'*

Actually, the Lord had not taken away; Satan had, but Job did not know the backstory, for he was not present in the courtroom that day.

²² In all this, Job did not sin nor charge God with wrong.

In all this, Job may have lost the stuff, but he did not lose the crowns. That is why Satan returned at the next court date.

Round 2

Job 2:1-10:

*¹ Again there was a day when the sons of God came to present themselves before the LORD, and Satan came also among them to present himself before the LORD. ² And the LORD said to Satan, <u>'From where do you come?'</u> Satan answered the LORD and said, **'From going to and fro on the earth, and from walking back and forth on it.'** (Emphasis mine)*

Again, Satan was looking for crowns to steal.

*³ Then the LORD said to Satan, 'Have you considered My servant Job, (he has crowns—a bunch of them) that there is none like him on the earth, a blameless and upright man, one who fears God (he had a Crown of the Fear of the Lord) and shuns evil? And still, **he holds fast to his integrity** (he also had a Crown of Integrity), although you incited Me against him, to destroy him <u>without cause.</u>'*

⁴ So Satan answered the LORD and said, 'Skin for skin! Yes, all that a man has he will give for his life. (false accusation) ⁵ But stretch out Your hand now, and touch his bone and his flesh, and he will surely curse You to Your face!' (false accusation)

⁶ And the LORD said to Satan, 'Behold, he is in your hand but <u>spare his life</u>.' (Emphasis mine)

The LORD again permitted Satan to affect Job.

⁷ So Satan went out from the presence of the LORD and struck Job with painful boils from the sole of his foot to the crown of his head. ⁸ And he took for himself a potsherd with which to scrape himself while he sat in the midst of the ashes.

⁹ Then his wife said to him, 'Do you still hold fast to your (crown of) integrity? Curse God and die!'

¹⁰ But he said to her, 'You speak as one of the foolish women speaks. Shall we indeed accept good from God, and shall we not accept adversity?' In all this, <u>Job did not sin with his lips</u>. (Emphasis mine)

This was an attempt to steal Job's Crown of Integrity. The enemy afflicted his health but failed to steal the crown.

Restoration Comes

Job 42:10-17:

*¹⁰ And the LORD restored Job's losses when he prayed for his friends. Indeed, **the LORD gave Job twice as much as he had before.***

¹¹ Then all his brothers, all his sisters, and all those who had been his acquaintances before, came to him and ate food with him in his house; and they consoled him and comforted him for all the adversity that the LORD had brought upon him. Each one gave him a piece of silver and each a ring of gold.

*¹² Now **the LORD blessed the latter days of Job more than his beginning**; for he had fourteen thousand sheep, six thousand camels, one thousand yoke of oxen, and one thousand female donkeys. ¹³ He also had seven sons and three daughters. ¹⁴ And he called the name of the first Jemimah, the name of the second Keziah, and the name of the third Keren-Happuch.*

¹⁵ In all the land were found no women so beautiful as the daughters of Job; and their father gave them an inheritance among their brothers.

¹⁶ After this, Job lived one hundred forty years and saw his children and grandchildren for four generations.

17 So Job died, old and full of days. (Emphasis mine)

All the dominion the crowns possessed was restored to him in the end.

Joshua, the High Priest and the Restoration of His Crown

Zechariah 3:1-10:

1 Then he showed me Joshua the high priest standing before the Angel of the LORD, and **Satan standing at his right hand to oppose him.**

2 And the LORD said to Satan, 'The LORD rebuke you, Satan! The LORD who has chosen Jerusalem rebuke you! Is this not a brand plucked from the fire'

3 Now Joshua was clothed with filthy garments, and was standing before the Angel.

4 Then He answered and spoke to those who stood before Him, saying, 'Take away the filthy garments from him.' And to him He said, 'See, I have removed your iniquity from you, and I will clothe you with rich robes.' 5 And I said, 'Let them put a clean turban on his head.' So they put a clean turban on his head, and they put the clothes on him. And the Angel of the LORD stood by.

⁶ Then the Angel of the LORD admonished Joshua, saying, ⁷ 'Thus says the LORD of hosts: "If you will walk in My ways, and if you will keep My command, then you shall also judge My house, and likewise have charge of My courts; I will give you places to walk among these who stand here.

⁸ "Hear, O Joshua, the high priest, You and your companions who sit before you, for they are a wondrous sign; for behold, I am bringing forth My Servant the BRANCH. ⁹ For behold, the stone that I have laid before Joshua: upon the stone are seven eyes. Behold, I will engrave its inscription," says the LORD of hosts, "And I will remove the iniquity of that land in one day. ¹⁰ In that day," says the LORD of hosts, "Everyone will invite his neighbor under his vine and under his fig tree."' (Emphasis mine)

The accusation was that Joshua was disqualified from serving as High Priest due to the condition of his garments. The LORD superseded Satan by replacing his garments and preparing him to be crowned. In Zechariah 6:11-14, we read:

*¹¹ Take the silver and gold, make **an elaborate crown**, and set it on the head of Joshua the son of Jehozadak, the high priest. ¹² Then speak to* *him, saying, 'Thus says the LORD of hosts, saying: 'Behold, the Man whose name is the BRANCH! From His place He shall branch out, and He shall build the temple of the LORD;*

¹³ Yes, He shall build the temple of the LORD. He shall bear the glory, and shall sit and rule on His throne; so He shall be a priest on His throne, and the counsel of peace shall be between them both.'
¹⁴ 'Now the elaborate crown shall be for a memorial in the temple of the LORD for Helem, Tobijah, Jedaiah, and Hen the son of Zephaniah.'

He had been prepared for the crown in chapter 3 but was finally crowned in chapter 7.

Sometimes preparation time is necessary before the coronation with a crown.

Satan's Pattern

Satan's jealousy of the sons is proven in the theft of the righteousness, peace, and authority that the sons must reign in.

He corrupts the crowns by misappropriating them.

Your first measure is to understand the depth that he has gone to steal, kill, and destroy *in AND with* the removal of the Crown of Authority.

Each of the crowns given by Heaven are Crowns of Authority.

When Satan steals your crown, he usurps your authority.

Usurping authority is when one tries to take another's position or authority away by force.

When the enemy steals your crown, he is usurping the authority that the crown represents.

Each of us has been given realms of authority.

This is what happened to Elijah after he slew the prophets of Baal. Once Elijah had slain the 450 prophets of Baal, he received a Crown of Authority over Baal. Jezebel had not permitted her 400 prophets of Asherah to attend the showdown with Elijah (although that was the instruction given to Ahab). She was concerned that

Elijah might also defeat her prophets and destroy them, so she sought to bully him and cause him to surrender his Crown of Authority.[6]

1 Kings 19:1-18:

> *[1] And Ahab told Jezebel all that Elijah had done, also how he had executed all the prophets with the sword. [2] Then Jezebel sent a messenger to Elijah, saying, 'So let the gods do to me, and more also, if I do not make your life as the life of one of them by tomorrow about this time.'*
>
> *[3] And* **when he <u>saw</u> that, he arose and ran for his life,** *and went to Beersheba, which belongs to Judah, and left his servant there. (Emphasis mine)*

Elijah feared for his life, and at that moment, he surrendered his crown. Depression, defeat, and despair are earmarks of a lost crown, and you will see them played out in a moment.

> *[4] But he himself went a day's journey into the wilderness and came and sat down under a broom tree. And he prayed that he might die and said, 'It is enough! Now, LORD, take my life, for I am no better than my fathers!'*

---

[6] 1 Kings 19:18-20

Elijah has suicidal thoughts because of his despair and depression.

His First Angelic Visitation:

⁵ Then, as he lay and slept under a broom tree, suddenly an angel touched him and said to him, 'Arise and eat.'

Elijah needed to eat. He was hungry and dehydrated. His fatigue was contributing to his depression. Dehydration can affect your ability to perceive spiritually.

*⁶ Then he looked, and there by his head was a cake baked on coals and a jar of water. So **he ate and drank** and **lay down again.***

Sometimes, you just need to do something that seems totally unspiritual: rest.

His Second Angelic Visitation:

*⁷ And the angel of the LORD came back **the second time**, and **touched him, and said**, 'Arise and eat, because the journey is too great for you.'*

Once refreshed, Elijah needed the touch of Heaven. He was instructed to eat again because he was still undernourished. Once sufficiently refreshed, he was ready to go on the next part of his journey. **He had his crown back.**

> *⁸ So he arose and ate and drank; and he went in the strength of that food forty days and forty nights as far as Horeb, the mountain of God.*
>
> *⁹ And there he went into a cave, and spent the night in that place; and behold, the word of the LORD came to him, and He said to him, '**<u>What are you doing here, Elijah?</u>**' (Emphasis mine)*

This is the first time he has been asked this question. How did the Word of the LORD come to him?

He didn't yet have the full strength of his crown but was making progress. It carried him for 40 days and nights.

> *¹⁰ So <u>he said, 'I have been very zealous for the LORD God of hosts</u>; for the children of Israel have forsaken Your covenant, torn down Your altars, and killed Your prophets with the sword. I alone am left; and they seek to take my life.'*

Often, when we are tired or depressed, we begin to moan and operate in self-pity. His instruction from the Lord was to go out and stand on the mountain of the LORD.

> *¹¹ Then He said, '<u>Go out, and stand on the mountain before the LORD</u>.' And behold, the LORD passed by, and a great and strong wind tore into the mountains and broke the rocks in*

*pieces before the LORD, but the LORD was not in the wind, and after the wind an earthquake, but the LORD was not in the earthquake; ^{12} and after the earthquake a fire, but the LORD was not in the fire; and after the fire **a still small voice**.*

*^{13} So it was, when Elijah heard it, that **he wrapped his face in his mantle** and went out and stood in the entrance of the cave. Suddenly, a voice came to him and said, '**What are you doing here, Elijah?**' (Emphasis mine)*

He heard the same question and gave the same answer to the LORD.

^{14} And <u>he said, 'I have been very zealous for the LORD God of hosts</u>; because the children of Israel have forsaken Your covenant, torn down Your altars, and killed Your prophets with the sword. I alone am left; and they seek to take my life.'

His second instruction:

*^{15} Then the LORD said to him: 'Go, return on your way to the Wilderness of Damascus; and when you arrive, **anoint Hazael as king over Syria**.'*

His instruction involved preparing **Hazael for his crown** and **Jehu for his crown.**

The anointing came BEFORE the crown was placed.

> *The anointing prepares you for the crown.*

¹⁶ 'Also, you shall **anoint Jehu the son of Nimshi as king over Israel.** And Elisha the son of Shaphat of Abel Meholah, you shall anoint as prophet in your place.'

He was to anoint his replacement, also. The anointing is to destroy those who oppose God's purposes.

God designed a three-pronged defense.

¹⁷ 'It shall be that whoever escapes **the sword of Hazael, Jehu** will kill; and whoever escapes the sword of Jehu, **Elisha** will kill.

¹⁸ Yet I have reserved seven thousand in Israel, all whose knees have not bowed to Baal, and every mouth that has not kissed him.'

The Second Book:
The Mirror of Crowns

We were then directed to the second book. This book had no image on the front, and Mary explained that the reason for that was that it was each son's Book of Crowns.

We each have a Book of Crowns.

This is a picture of your crowns and the crowns you've lost. It's like a record—a registry of sorts.

The picture will appear as you move in this understanding and take your crowns back. Pictures come in many forms regarding the Books of Crowns but consider it an authority for the sake of understanding. We understood that it would not be an actual picture in the book.

---
*It is the concept of the authority
we walk in that will be made known.*

Mary had Stephanie open the book. Stephanie asked, "What do I do from here, Mary?"

It was a mirror. As she held the mirror, she could see her crowns.

Mary explained, "The mirror image and reflection of the crowns you wear are pictured here as a record of sorts. Know that it delights Him to sit with you and have you mirror the crowns He has given you as it brings Him much delight.

> *The value and importance
> of retrieving crowns will be displayed
> as a mirror reflection of how
> you walk in your authority as a son.*

To understand that each crown represents an area of one's life in which one has experienced victory is to understand that it is one less area the enemy has to confront you successfully in. Also, when you receive victory in an area, you are then empowered to teach others how to receive victory in that same area; thus, reducing Satan's dominion in people's lives.

> *Once you receive a particular crown,
> he may attempt to steal it from you,
> but you can learn to walk in a grace
> that makes his attempts futile
> against your life.*

The Third Book:

The Royal Priesthood of the Crown

The third book is called *The Royal Priesthood of the Crown*. We know we are kings and priests, but Stephanie was not privy to open it yet. However, insights were granted later and are in a later chapter.

With that, our engagement ended. We thanked Mary for her assistance, saying, "Thank you, Father. Thank you, Jesus. Mary. I look forward to more of an understanding of the revelation of the mirroring and the kings and priests, royal priesthood of the crowns of the records. We will know. Thank you for this clarity."

———— ∞ ————

Chapter 4
The Crown of Crowns

Stephanie described our next engagement: "I see the same three books across the table from me. Someone has brought in what looks like a tablecloth, but they're putting it over the large table in front of us." It even covered the top of the three books, with crowns from left to right. They were in order. She first noticed three magnificent crowns directly on the left, and they were stacked on top of one another. Next to them were smaller crowns, seven of which were placed in a row. Then, one large crown in the middle.

Then there was a row of five crowns, but they were two stacked on top of one another, five in a row. The last one doesn't look like a crown, but we thought it must be since it was on this table of crowns. It looked more like a giant gold necklace that covered the width of the table, and it had gold strands hanging from it and hanging off the table.

"Where do you want us to start?" we wondered. "What is the purpose of this?"

"These are different inflections of crowns," our tutor replied.

Stephanie asked, "What's an inflection?"

I answered, "It's a change in the form of a word, typically to the ending, to express a grammatical function or attributes such as tense, mood, person, number, case, or gender."

Stephanie remarked, "Apparently, we're looking at numbers of crowns. Our tutor is making me focus on the crown in the middle, which is so large. It's almost the table's width, and its circumference is the same all the way around."

"What crown is this?" We asked.

Our tutor replied:

This is His crown that all other crowns come from.

Stephanie had a picture of a father playing with a little boy, his son. The father is a king and just in play, because he loves his son. The son wanted to wear the crown, so he took it off his head and put it on the little boy. it slipped over the little boy's head and rested on his shoulders. It was a loving picture. Then, Heaven showed her a quick clip of when we died with Him, and now we are raised with Him. She heard, "**From this crown comes all the other crowns,** but *we have access to this crown too.*"

From this crown comes all the other crowns, but we have access to this crown, too.

Mary (the mother of Jesus) came into the room. We greeted her, and she climbed on the table and sat inside the crown. She asked Stephanie to join her.

Stephanie joined her in the crown and noted, "Nothing spectacular happened when I sat down with her, but as I sit here, I can see this crown from inside it all the way around. Wow! It's big enough that, as I am seated, it is coming past my head while I sit crisscross applesauce. There is an inscription inside the crown of <u>all</u> our names."

Mary had her look closer, and Stephanie said, "It's not an inscription; it is an indentation. I can put my finger into the indentation of my name on this crown of gold."

Mary told us that we see each of our names on the crown because we are part of it. She explained, "This is the source of our identity in Him. We are *in* this crown indentation with our name."

The Word says we are in Him. There were so many names indented on the crown. Mary said that He allowed us to take hold of this crown, and she reached over, touched, and grasped the outer part of it. Then, Stephanie came and touched it, too.

Mary said, "As this sits upon His head, the memory of you and everything about you floods His mind and His heart, and that is how He has created the crown to work. But most people don't realize that His very thoughts of them are innumerable, just like the number of names I see here.[7] We've been taught 'what's mine is mine and what's yours is yours,' but in this space—in this place, this belongs to Him *and* us."

Hebrews 2:6:

> *Somewhere in the Scriptures it is written, 'What is it about the human species that* **God cannot get them out of his mind?** *What does he see in the son of man, that so captivates his gaze?'* *(MIRROR) (Emphasis mine)*

We watched as Mary saw her name, took her fingers, and placed them inside the indentation of her name. Her fingers went deep into the crown.

Stephanie searched for her name and began to realize that our name's inscription here was unique to

---

[7] Psalms 40:5 Many, O LORD my God, are Your wonderful works which You have done; and Your thoughts toward us cannot be recounted to You in order; if I would declare and speak of them, they are more than can be numbered.

each of us—how He views us and feels about us. Stephanie was checking to see her name and at the end of it, there was a heart inscribed after her name. We are told to inscribe His words and His name upon *our* hearts. This is a picture of how our name is inscribed upon His heart.[8]

She was leaning over due to the way this crown was shaped; it has long indentions upward, and then it comes down to a smaller part where there is a jewel on the opposite side and then a more extended part. Mary grabbed it and leaned up against it. With a big smile on her face, she said, **"This is where people need to start to understand the effects of the crowns and what they are and what they represent—to know that:**

> *He wears the crown with the*
> *very inscription of your name—*
> *the indentation of your name.*

"His thoughts are constantly of you,[9] and that **this crown is also ours** because of everything He has given us. It is the nature of the king to bestow these things

---

[8] See Proverbs 7:3 Bind them on your fingers; write them on the tablet of your heart.

[9] Psalms 139:17-18 [17] How precious also are Your thoughts to me, O God! How great is the sum of them! [18] If I should count them, they would be more in number than the sand; When I awake, I am still with You.

upon His sons instantaneously, and they become a crown." It was small enough that I could see hers on her head. She then gave me my crown to put on my head. With that, Mary walked away, and our engagement ended. Yet, we knew we would return.

——————— ∞ ———————

Chapter 5
Your Crown of Authority

As we engaged Heaven this day, Ezekiel presented himself. It was as if he were in a movie, and he leaned out of the screen and told us he was part of the storyline.

Stephanie asked, "What is the storyline today?" She began to see a great battle, and she realized it was a cosmic one. They showed her the background. She could see different cosmic dimensions, and Ezekiel stood in front of what we would view as a star, a brightly lit star. He took his sword and pierced it. It was the Bright and Morning Star. As he did so, a liquid poured forth that appeared pure in its form, with gold and white elements flowing out. As it poured out, the star seemed to collapse.

Ezekiel moved up to a host of other angels that Stephanie began to see. There were millions and millions of angels. She realized that the liquid pouring from the star was falling onto the Earth and into the crowns on their heads. As the last drops of liquid from the star fell onto the Earth, they covered the entire planet. She could hear a shout that the angels had shouted as they came full force towards the Earth. She could see them piercing the atmosphere as they fought in the heavens. She could see from the perspective on Earth that we, the sons, with these crowns filled with oil—this light and gold—had our hands outstretched, and we were praying and speaking to the atmosphere with authority as if the words we spoke empowered the angels.

Stephanie asked, "What is this about?"

Lady Wisdom (who had joined us) said, "These crowns are vessels upon your heads. The crowns—they are vessels. Supernatural outpourings go *into* these crowns that are upon your heads. Each one is unique to the individual."

Stephanie commented, "I am seeing that although we may have crowns with the same name, what is poured out to the individual and upon their head, filling this crown, is unique to that individual. Will you give me clarity, Ezekiel, on this picture I am seeing? At the beginning of this engagement, I heard you say, 'Great War.' I thought it was the war before humans were put on the Earth, but it's not."

The Spirit of Wisdom came up beside her and took Stephanie by her left hand.

Stephanie said, "Wisdom, tell me and help me understand what this picture represents."

Wisdom replied, "This is the picture of the uniqueness of each crown. The outpouring and the infilling of Jesus into the crown. Just as unique as the relationship each has with the Trinity, so is the uniqueness of what is poured out to the individual.

A diversity among the crowns exists as well as a diversity of the outpouring.

"If each of you carried the same anointing, there would be no use for the body. Discover what has been poured out. The discovery is in the unique intimacy with the Trinity. Jesus, who has poured himself out, is one piece of this.

What do you carry?

"View this in the aspect of the crown on your head, for we know it is not in and of yourselves, but what He has given. See the perspective from the crown. These are the mysteries that are being unfolded to the sons."

Stephanie remarked, "Wisdom told me to ask, 'What is the uniqueness that I carry in my crown?' You are to ask." So, I asked the Trinity—the Father, Son, and Holy

Spirit, 'What is the unique pouring out that you have put in my crown?'"

Stephanie continued, "For me, Holy Spirit told me He has given me a specific flavor of speaking that is unique to the Kingdom, a *unique personalization*. The Father said He's given me *a specific authorization*. Jesus said He's given me *a specific organization*.

"How is it unique for the Kingdom?"

- Pause and ask the Trinity: "What is the unique outpouring that you have for my crown?"
- Pause and ask the Father: "What is the unique authorization of my Crown of Authority?"
- Ask Jesus: "What is the specific organization of my crown?"
- And ask Holy Spirit: "What is the unique personalization of my Crown of Authority?"

[If necessary, pause and pray in the spirit before and after each question. These are some of the mysteries Heaven is revealing in this time.]

Stephanie remarked, "They are showing me the crown on top of my head, which is full of the outpoured liquid, and that as I live, move, and have my being in Jesus, I walk in this authorization, organization, and unique personalization; it spills out of this crown." Do you know how, when you walk with a cup of coffee, it's too full and spills over? It looks like that. This is your Crown of Authority.

"It is because it's not *our* authority. This is a picture *OF* authority."

Holy Spirit said, "The authority *in <u>and</u> from* this crown is unique to each person. **Every person walks in a *specific authority* that is different and unique from others.**"

The authority in and from this crown is what is unique to each person.

Everyone has a Crown of Authority.

It is what is being poured into that crown, be it from hell or Heaven, that is unique to the individual.

What are you making your source to draw from?

Stephanie said, "I'm seeing a different picture now of the princes and the powers of this Earth pouring out a vile liquid into the Crowns of Authority of those who walk in darkness."

Holy Spirit said, "**The reason you have a Crown of Authority from the moment of your birth is because you are *from and out of* the Father.** You are *from* and *out of* His original creation, uniqueness and design."

You are from and out of His original creation, uniqueness, and design.

Stephanie commented, "I see us as babies with this little crown on our head, and that's what the enemy seeks to defile, this specific Crown of Authority that Christ places on us at birth. We rule and reign."

The enemy seeks to defile this specific Crown of Authority.

If the crown can be defiled, it removes the authority of the sons.

Satan fears when we walk with the heavenly anointing poured into the crown's authority.

That is why I initially saw the picture of us all outside with these crowns on. We were speaking, praising, and walking in authority.

> *We are a part of changing the Earth.*

We are a part of assisting angels. We are a part of it all. We are kings and priests. We can be kings and priests for the Kingdom of Heaven or kings and priests to the kingdom of darkness. Satan fell because he saw us in the future and was extremely upset about it. He was upset that the sons were given more authority than he was.

Hebrews 1:5-6 says:

> *⁵ For to which of the angels did He ever say: 'You are my son, today I have begotten you?' And again: 'I will be to him a Father, and he shall be to me a son?'*

> *⁶ But when He again brings the firstborn into the world, He says: 'Let all the angels of God worship Him.'*

> *God never gave authority to angels like he gives to sons.*

Satan did not like his job placement as lead worshipper in Heaven. He wanted the authority the sons had. That dissatisfaction resulted in the rebellion, where one-third of the angels fell.

What we say in the spiritual realm truly does matter, and it assists the angels in many ways. They have great strength, and they do things, but *we* carry the authority.

Stephanie recalled, "Holy Spirit, for as long as I can remember, since I was little, I've had dreams, or I've heard the enemy's voice say that I have no authority."

Holy Spirit asked, "Were you convinced of that?"

Stephanie admitted, "I think I was."

Holy Spirit said, "Then he succeeded."

Wisdom asked, "Do you believe you have authority now?"

Stephanie replied, "Yes, yes, I do. I'll take this image with me when ministering to someone, this crown that spills out the Glory, this crown that spills out all of Him! That is a good picture for me and a reminder that nothing is in and of myself, but I do have the Crown of Authority that He has given me, that He is inside of."

Being led to Revelation 3, Stephanie read from the Mirror Bible:

> [2] *Awake from your slumber. Get a firm grip on what little life you have left in you. Your work does not mirror my finished work.* [3] *Remember, therefore, what it felt like when you first heard and embraced the word as your own. It was like discovering a priceless treasure (like a crown). Now make up your mind once and for all. Why should I surprise you like a thief and break into*

your space whilst you are fast asleep and not even anticipating my intimate intent; not knowing the moment of my visitation?

*⁴ Yet you do have a few individual names in Sardis who have **not forgotten their true identity and soiled their garments.** They are those **who walk with me in innocence** and **who mirror the reference of their worth to be equal to my estimate of them.** ⁵ Everyone who sees their victory in me, I will clothe in white garments and they will realize that I am not in the business of fulfilling their law and performance based fears by blotting out their names from the Book of Life. Instead, I'm the one who endorses their identity face-to-face before my father and his celestial shepherd messengers.*

⁶ Now listen up with your inner ears. Hear with understanding what the spirit is saying to the ecclesia. ⁷ And to the messenger of the ecclesia of Philadelphia write: I am the holy and true one. I hold the key of David as prophesied in Isaiah 22:22. Yes, I unlock the mysteries of the heavenly dimensions and no one can shut the door and I lock the entrance and none can access it. ⁸ I am fully aware of your efforts in doing the work of the ministry. I want you to see something I have given you a doorway right in front of you that has been fully opened into the heavenly dimensions. Nothing can possibly close it again. Even when you have very little strength, you have treasured my word and have not contradicted my name.

⁹ Behold, the Jewish disguise will be exposed to be the synagogue of Satan. They have sourced their gatherings and accusations, but now I give them to you and will cause them to come face to face with you in fellowship and acknowledgement of my love, which I have bestowed upon you. ¹⁰ You have greatly valued the prophetic word which came to fulfillment in what I endured. I will also guard you with great care, empowering you to stand strong in the midst of the troubled times that are about to come upon the inhabited world to scrutinize the dwellers of the Earth.

¹¹ Do not let tough times make me seem distant from you. I am at hand. See my nearness, not my absence, and don't let temporal setbacks diminish your authority either. **Remember that you call the shots, you wear the crown. My crown endorses your crown. Let nothing take your crown.** *He is the king of kings and Lord of lords, not the king of slaves. He redeems his life from the pit and weaves the crown for him out of loving and kindness and tender mercies. ¹² It is in your individual continual association with your victory in me that I will* *make you to be like a strong pillar in the inner shrine of God's sanctuary, supporting the entire structure of my God habitation within you, a place to be your permanent abode from which you will never have to depart. I will engrave upon you the name of my God. Also, I want to know the name of the city of my God, the new Jerusalem that descends from Heaven, and my own new name. And to the celestial shepherd messenger of the Ecclesia, he who speaks is the Amen. He's the ultimate evidence and the one who defines faith. He personifies truth. She is the very source of God's creation.'* [13] *Now listen up with your inner ears. Hear with understanding what the Spirit is saying to the ecclesia.* [14] *And to the celestial shepherd-messenger of the ecclesia in Laodicea write: he who speaks in the amen.* ***He is the ultimate evidence and the one who defines faith; he personifies the truth,*** *she (Lady Wisdom) is the very source of God's creation. (MIRROR) (Emphasis and additions mine)*

In Proverbs 8:12-32 we find that Wisdom was at the beginning, at creation:

[12] *I, wisdom, dwell with prudence, and find out knowledge and discretion.* [13] *The fear of the LORD is to hate evil; pride and arrogance and the evil way and the perverse mouth I hate.* [14] *Counsel is mine, and sound wisdom; I am*

understanding, I have strength. ¹⁵ By me kings reign, And rulers decree justice. ¹⁶ By me princes rule, and nobles, all the judges of the earth. ¹⁷ I love those who love me, and those who seek me diligently will find me. ¹⁸ Riches and honor are with me, enduring riches and righteousness. ¹⁹ My fruit is better than gold, yes, than fine gold, and my revenue than choice silver. ²⁰ I traverse the way of righteousness, in the midst of the paths of justice, ²¹ That I may cause those who love me to inherit wealth, that I may fill their treasuries.

²² "The LORD possessed me at the beginning of His way, before His works of old. ²³ I have been established from everlasting, from the beginning, before there was ever an earth. ²⁴ When there were no depths I was brought forth, when there were no fountains abounding with water.

²⁵ Before the mountains were settled, before the hills, I was brought forth; ²⁶ While as yet He had not made the earth or the fields, or the primal dust of the world. ²⁷ **When He prepared the heavens, I was there**, when He drew a circle on the face of the deep, ²⁸ When He established the clouds above, when He strengthened the fountains of the deep, ²⁹ When He assigned to the sea its limit, so that the waters would not transgress His command, when He marked out

> *the foundations of the earth,* **³⁰ Then I was beside Him as a master craftsman; and I was daily His delight, rejoicing always before Him,** *³¹ Rejoicing in His inhabited world, and my delight was with the sons of men.*
>
> *³² Now therefore, listen to me, my children, for blessed are those who keep my ways. (Emphasis mine)*

For anyone who believes they are too small or have done too much that has been wrong, *the crown came from the Father when He created us* and when we choose to be filled with the goodness of the Bright and Morning Star. With the authority that He has given us, we don't ever have to worry about that again.

I'm excited. As the people begin praying for this, the great mystery of the individual anointing and authority on their life will unfold as they discover what that is.

Stephanie asked, "Ezekiel, what is the picture of what you pierced with your sword?"

Ezekiel replied, "He was pierced for your transgressions."

Isaiah 53:5:

> *But he was **pierced for our rebellion (transgression)**, crushed for our sins. He was beaten so we could be whole. He was whipped so we could be healed. (Emphasis mine)*

Stephanie continued, "Yeah, but that's what Ezekiel keeps saying. He was pierced. That's why what he did created this anointing for all the sons."

Ezekiel added, "This is your original design."

Stephanie remarked, "So, the picture is not you piercing this. He was pierced, and you are just showing us a picture of what happened on the cross. This is much more profound than what we thought.

Wisdom added, "The pouring out is celestial, is supernatural, it is dimensional, and it's a picture of the unique authorization and filling of our crowns to walk in the authority, boldness and execution of our sonship on this Earth."

Stephanie added, "I saw so many angels when Ezekiel pierced it, and then he went up, and he was with these millions of angels, and they came warring down upon the Earth, fighting the principalities and powers of the air, co-laboring with the ecclesia.

Thank You, Heaven. Thank You, Father, and thank You, Jesus. I ask that for every person that hears this message and they ask for the mystery for themselves, the uniqueness of what You have poured into their Crown of Authority, that they are empowered in their heart and their mind, realizing that this lie that we've all believed— that we have no authority, is dismantled forever.

Thank You, Jesus, that You were poured out and overcame our transgressions so we might walk in the authority as sons. Thank You, Wisdom, for being present from the beginning.

―――― · ――――

Chapter 6

The Crown of Sonship

Three people met us as we engaged Heaven in the Library of Revelation. As before, we sat at a large table. One of them was placing items on the table. She placed twelve pieces of shewbread (also known as "The Bread of His Presence") on the table, joining the wine and bread already laid out. Two candlesticks were also on the table. We were instructed to sit down. Shewbread was twelve loaves placed every Sabbath in the Jewish temple and eaten by the priests at the end of the week. It means *presence bread*.

One of the people stepped into view, a woman who began putting twelve crowns on the table, one at each seat. Stephanie understood that this person was Mary, the one who washed Jesus' feet and anointed Him with her hair.

As Stephanie looked at the crown before her, she asked what it was known as and was told it was the

Crown of Sonship. Once the crown was placed on her head, Mary began speaking, "With the Crown of Sonship displayed for all to see, it's an open invitation to sit at the table. Sonship is represented. The shewbread represents His presence. It's an open invitation to His presence.

"Many believe they cannot enter His presence. The Crown of Sonship is a picture *and* a spiritual reality of our sonship."

This crown is a representation of how we, as sons, do not walk in a sin-conscious manner.

Stephanie said, "So, what I'm understanding is when people realize they can put this crown on (it's so good that Heaven is allowing us to see something that's spiritual visually), it doesn't matter what we have done in the past, but rather, because they believe in Him, they can stand in the fact that He died for our sins once and for all. As we do this work, we can be in His presence with this sonship crown—His very presence. We can eat of Him and drink of Him. We're invited to sit at His table. He's prepared a table for us in the presence of our enemies, but we're invited to sit with Him, to be in His presence. Am I right, Mary?"

Mary asked, "What did He do for me when I washed His feet and poured out the anointing oil upon Him?"

"In your brokenness, in front of everyone who was making fun of you and being angry at wasting something, He honored you," Stephanie answered.

Mary responded, "That's right.

---

*Sonship entails honor
by being given a Crown of Sonship.*

"The Most High is honoring the sons, in spite of you and despite how *YOU* feel about YOU.

---

*Your position is to honor
the Kingdom by having a seat
in His presence.*

"It's an invitation, an open one."

Stephanie asked, "What do the two candlesticks represent?"

"Intimacy."

"She showed me a picture of a husband and wife sitting at a candlelit dinner. That's what this is," Stephanie explained.

Mary shared some other things that it is not time to disclose, but in closing, she said:

> Learning about the crowns will increase government upon the Earth.

1 Peter 1:2-3:

² Your original identity is defined by what God, the Father of mankind has always cherished about you; knowing that your pre-Adamic innocence in spirit, would be preserved in the prophetic word, and redeemed through the obedience of Jesus Christ, and the effect of the sprinkling of his blood. Realizing his grace and peace exceeds any definition of contradiction or reward. ³ Let us celebrate the God and Father of our Lord Jesus Christ with articulate acclaim. According to his matchless mercy and tender compassions, he birthed us again when Jesus was raised from the dead. In him, we were rebooted to live the authentic life of our design; while participating in a living hope, witnessing the Father's expectation of the ages unfold in us. (MIRROR)

1 Peter 3:18:

Christ died once and for all in order to conclusively separate you from a distorted identity. Thus, restored righteousness [shared likeness] triumphed beyond the reach of any identity that is not in sync with innocence and oneness, [righteousness bringing closure to unrighteousness]— in order that he might lead you-manity to be face to face with God; his body was murdered, but he was made alive in spirit. ¹⁹ Thus, through the doorway of death, his spirit entered the very domain where those who died before were imprisoned. There, he announced his message. ²⁰ There is a new baptism. Immersed in his death and co-quickened in his resurrection, mankind once dead and drowned are now made alive and crowned. (MIRROR)

Psalm 8:5-6:

⁵ Yet you made him little less than God, [Elohim] and crowns him with glory and honor. ⁶ You have given him dominion over the works of your hands; you have put all things under his feet.] (MIRROR)

Luke 12:29-32:

*²⁹ **Your preoccupation with your daily needs neutralizes you**—it's like you're stuck in midair somewhere. ³⁰ **These things are the typical anxieties of every nation on the planet**—your Father is affectionately acquainted with you and knows exactly what you need. ³¹ Much rather pursue the extent of his royal influence and witness how all these things are provided by your Father. ³² You might sometimes feel so vulnerable and overwhelmed* *by the odds against you, like a fragile little flock of lambs amidst wolves. You have nothing to fear—it is your Father's delight to give you the Kingdom.*

*(See Revelation 3:11: Do not let tough times make me seem distant from you. I am at hand—see my nearness, not my absence. And don't let temporal setbacks **diminish your own authority, either. Remember that you call the shots; you wear the crown. My crown endorses your crown.** [Lit. **Let nothing take your crown.** (Revelation 1:5)*

Let nothing take your crown.

He is the King of kings and Lord of lords. Not King of slaves. (Revelation 19:16)

He redeems his life from the Pit and weaves a crown for him out of loving-kindness and tender mercies. (Psalm 103:4)

*[33] From now on, **do life from a different perspective. Stuff does not define you.** Exchange whatever it was that you've been doing all along under the old system of performance, for this new life of adventure. Get it over and done with. Be compassion driven in your sharing and giving; this takes hoarding out of the equation. Get rid of your antique purses*

(money bags), which typically are your old, worn-out, performance-based ideas. Instead, become creative in the adventure of trading with a new kind of purse—one that is loaded with heaven's currency—a treasure which cannot be exhausted, since it cannot be broken into or stolen, neither can it be ruined by moths. The stuff you've been hoarding before, are clearly targets for thieves and they get moth eaten anyway. This is the typical dilemma of a person whose treasure is reduced to his own ability to accumulate things for himself in order to define him, **rather than discovering his wealth in God.** *³⁴ The heart is naturally drawn to the place where one's treasure is. (MIRROR) (Luke 12:33-34) (Emphasis mine)*

Psalm 103:1-6:

¹ Bless Jahweh יהוה YHVH, oh my soul; and all that is within me, bless his holy name. ² Bless Jahweh, oh my soul, and forget not all his benefits, ³ who forgives all your iniquity, who heals all your diseases, ⁴ He redeems your life from the Pit and **weaves a crown for you out of loving-kindness and tender mercies.** *⁵ He satisfies you with good as long as you live so that your youth is renewed like the eagle's.) ⁶ He fashioned us into a kingdom of priests unto his God and Father. The glory and the* **ruling**

authority *of the ages belong to him for all time and eternity. Amen. (MIRROR) (Emphasis mine)*

Revelation 3:11-12:

¹¹ Do not let tough times make me seem distant from you. I am at hand—see my nearness, not my absence. And don't let temporal setbacks diminish your own authority either. Remember that you call the shots; you wear the crown. ***My crown endorses your crown.***

¹² It is in your individual, continual association with your victory in me that I will make you to be like a strong pillar in the inner shrine of God's sanctuary, supporting the entire structure of my God-habitation within you. A place to be your permanent abode from whence you will never have to depart. And I will engrave upon you the name of my God, also the name of the city [the bride.] of my God, the new Jerusalem that descends from heaven; as well as my own new Name. (MIRROR) (Emphasis mine)

As sons embrace their sonship they will find themselves living in an entirely new way.

Much of the past teachings we learned from organized religion will be cleared away, making room for more of the Father's goodness to manifest in our lives.

---
*Welcome the changes
and wear your Crown of Sonship
with gratitude to the Father.*

∞

Chapter 7
The Crown of Everlasting

As we engaged Heaven, Malcolm and Lydia stood in the same place, so we asked, "What do you want us to learn?"

Malcolm answered, "There's also a Crown of Everlasting. When you carry the Crown of Discernment, are astute, and understand the Crown of Everlasting, you will know that the gifts that are given to the sons are everlasting."

"Well, that's good, Malcolm," Stephanie replied. "I was thinking you were talking about lasting forever."

Malcolm quipped, "Oh, there's much more beyond that."

The Crown of Everlasting is widespread.

"What does that mean? Stephanie asked.

He then showed her a picture of Jesus in the manger and said, "Who is this, the King of Glory?"

"It's Jesus."

"Is He from everlasting?"

"Yes," we replied.

He went on, "Are you not sons from everlasting?"

"Yes, we are."

"Then pick up your Crown of Everlasting, which is widespread (meaning you don't have to look for it. The Crowns of Everlasting are scattered all around you). Pick it up. Pick up the crown."

As Stephanie reached for the Crown of Everlasting, the baby she had seen in the crib—Jesus—handed the crown to her to put on.

As she placed it on her head, she could feel the Holy Spirit all over her head, especially the top of her head. She understood that it was widespread because that was what He brought with the cost of His life. The cost that anyone would bear is nothing compared to the price He paid for this widespread Crown of Everlasting. She began to see many crowns on the Earth, scattered on the ground—they were everywhere.

Malcolm instructed us to pick them up and said, "You can use them and put them upon the heads of your loved ones, ones who don't know Him as sons. You can position Him on their heads. This is what He paid for.

This is what He did there. They are everlasting, and they are widespread."

Stephanie began picking up the crowns and placed them on the heads of her family prophetically, then upon others that she knew and loved.

"This is evangelism. This is truth," Malcolm spoke.

She then prayed,

In the name of Jesus, for my daughters, for my brother, where they gave their crowns away, where they dropped them, or where it was stolen from them, I repent on their behalf. Where I may even have knocked them off their heads, I repent. I ask for the blood of Jesus and the amendment of 'As if it Never Were.'

In the Court of Crowns, I request this amendment as these crowns are placed on the heads of those that I will meet. (I see that I can do this for those that will come into my path). I pick up these crowns.

Stephanie began picking up some of the crowns she saw and put them on her arms like large bracelets. She knew that now that she had them, she could simply place them on the heads of those she meets that don't know the Lord, and it opens up the door because the cost that He paid has availed them.

She can place this Crown of Everlasting upon them because they are His children—they are the Father's sons. That's why the crowns were everywhere on the ground.

She continued to pray,

Thank you, Jesus that you provided a Crown of Everlasting for every single person.

As I see this and I am meeting a stranger in the future, one that doesn't look like me, one that doesn't act like me, but I have no judgment or condemnation towards them because I have a crown that you've given them. It's my job to put it upon their head. Thank you, Jesus.

Malcolm explained, "The authority in the Crowns of Discernment (which is astuteness) allows you to visualize and see the Crowns of Everlasting for those of your family members and those you will meet that are put upon your path of true evangelism for the Kingdom."

"How would Heaven have us do this?"

He replied, "If you are wearing a Crown of Discernment, have them be astute—bring the prodigals, bring everyone that doesn't follow Jesus. Pick up the crowns." (You will know in your spirit if they are the ones on whom to place a Crown of Everlasting.)

Stephanie explained what she was seeing: "I keep seeing me putting them on my arm like a bracelet. They were all the way up to my shoulders on both of my arms. As I put them on my family members and others that I love, as well as those who come across my path, I immediately understood that we may often ask for divine appointments, but **we *are* divine appointments to others.**

"Thank you, Lydia and Malcolm. Thank you, Father. You answered my prayer about discernment and gave me a different definition to better understand it.

Discernment is more than just discerning evil spirits. It's discerning who lost their crown, too.

"Thank you, Jesus. Thank you, Father. Thank you, Heaven."

Angels, I request that you help us in our discernment, our astuteness, to see the Crowns of Everlasting that are everywhere, to know when to pick it up or when to have one to help put on another one that needs the understanding and can receive Jesus and what He did for them.

———— ∞ ————

Chapter 8

Discovering

The Crown of Discernment

In this engagement, we requested more knowledge about crowns and Heaven did not disappoint.

As we stepped into Heaven, Stephanie immediately saw the men and women in white, with their crowns upon their heads, whom we regularly visit. Malcolm and Lydia again came forward.

Stephanie felt a crown on the top of her head and heard the word "astuteness." Astuteness is the ability to accurately assess situations or people and use the information to one's advantage.[10]

---

[10] Proverbs 14:18-19 18 The naïve demonstrate a lack of wisdom, but the lovers of wisdom are crowned with revelation-knowledge. 19 Evil ones will pay tribute to good people and eventually come to be servants of the godly. (TPT)

She was told she was wearing a Crown of Discernment. She had been asking for discernment and wondered if it was similar to astuteness and Heaven indicated that the Crown of Discernment *causes* astuteness.

Malcolm asked, "What is discernment?"

She immediately knew that you must accurately understand because the question in her mind was, "Can everyone have a Crown of Discernment?"

"Is it not to the son's advantage to have discernment?" Malcolm asked.

"Of course it is," we replied.

He elucidated, "Many have lost their Crown of Discernment."

Many have set it down because of fear, and many have given it away because of the cost.

He instructed, "Pick up your crowns, sons. The time is at hand. Discernment is what is necessary for such a time as this.

Be astute, carry the Flame of Discernment. It is in the crown.

Stephanie noted that the very first point of the crown had a flame in it. Then, she could feel the presence of the Holy Spirit in her body.

She remarked, "Thank you, Lord. I've been wanting to feel you. Thank you, Father. It is the Holy Spirit, and that is the Flame of Discernment. Thank you, Holy Spirit. I see you on this crown.

"I have an understanding about people who, because of fear, because of the perceived cost, have set their crowns down, and even given them away. There is repentance work regarding that, but once that is done, the Crown of Discernment is easily placed back on their head with the truth."

The cost isn't what you think.

———— ∞ ————

Chapter 9
Types of Crowns in Scripture
Part 1

The restoration of crowns is just the beginning. Many have lost territories that need to be restored. Others have lost inheritances that need restoration. Now that they have gone in and reclaimed their crowns have them step into the Court of Crowns and receive renewed authorization for the authority that had been lost. Explore this Court, for it is part of the retaking of lands and properties, gold, and treasure, all of which have been waiting for the sons to step into a new level of sonship in this day and hour. The thing which has been stolen needs to be reclaimed, and that is done sevenfold.

> *Remember, the crown one possesses represents the authority one possesses, and to de-crown you is to dethrone you.*

To dethrone you is to minimize your placement and your destiny, and your authority is given to another.

Understanding your loss of crowns has been the first step. Retrieving them is the next step, but understanding the authority is true revelation.

Revelation 3:11:

> *Behold, I am coming quickly! Hold fast what you have, that **no one may take your crown**.*

> *Each of us has been given realms of authority.*

Satan wants to steal YOUR crown. When Satan steals your crown, he usurps your authority.

> *Remember, the more crowns you remove from Satan's kingdom and take back as sons, the less authority in roaming he will have.*

> *The value and importance
> of retrieving the crowns will be
> displayed as a mirror reflection
> of how you walk
> in your authority as a son.*

In the Bible, there are several types of crowns that symbolize different aspects of reward, honor, and achievement in the Christian faith. Here are some of the key crowns mentioned:

Crown of Life

This crown is promised to those who endure trials and sufferings for the sake of Christ. It symbolizes perseverance through hardship and is often associated with martyrdom or enduring temptation. It is mentioned in James 1:12 and Revelation 2:10.

This crown is given to those who are faithful unto death.

James 1:12:

> *Blessed is the one who perseveres under trial because, having stood the test, that person will receive the **crown of life** that the Lord has promised to those who love him. (Emphasis mine)*

Revelation 2:8-11:

⁸ And to the angel of the church in Smyrna write, 'These things says the First and the Last, who was dead, and came to life:

*⁹ 'I know your works, tribulation, and poverty (but you are rich); and I know the blasphemy of those who say they are Jews and are not, but are a synagogue of Satan. ¹⁰ Do not fear any of those things which you are about to suffer. Indeed, the devil is about to throw some of you into prison, that you may be tested, and you will have tribulation ten days. <u>Be faithful until death,</u> and I will give you **the crown of life.** ¹¹ 'He who has an ear, let him hear what the Spirit says to the churches. He who overcomes shall not be hurt by the second death.' (Emphasis mine)*

Imperishable Crown

This crown is given to those who live disciplined and faithful lives, particularly those who exercise self-control in their spiritual walk. It is described as imperishable, unlike earthly crowns that fade away. 1 Corinthians 9:25 talks about this crown in the context of athletic discipline and self-mastery.

This crown is given to those who practice servanthood for the right reasons.

1 Corinthians 9:14-27:

¹⁴ Even so the Lord has commanded that those who preach the gospel should live from the gospel. ¹⁵ But I have used none of these things, nor have I written these things that it should be done so to me; for it would be better for me to die than that anyone should make my boasting void. ¹⁶ For if I preach the gospel, I have nothing to boast of, for necessity is laid upon me; yes, woe is me if I do not preach the gospel! ¹⁷ For if I do this willingly, I have a reward; but if against my will, I have been entrusted with a stewardship.

¹⁸ What is my reward then? That when I preach the gospel, I may present the gospel of Christ without charge, that I may not abuse my authority in the gospel. ¹⁹ For though I am free from all men, <u>I have made myself a servant to all</u>, that I might win the more; ²⁰ and to the Jews I became as a Jew, that I might win Jews; to those who are under the law, as under the law, that I might win those who are under the law; ²¹ to those who are without law, as without law (not being without law toward God, but under law toward Christ), that I might win those who are without law; ²² to the weak I became as weak, that I might win the weak. I have become all things to all men, that I might by all means save some.

²³ Now this I do for the gospel's sake, that I may be partaker of it with you. ²⁴ Do you not know that those who run in a race all run, but one receives the prize? Run in such a way that you may obtain it. ²⁵ *And everyone who competes for the prize is temperate in all things. Now they do it to obtain a perishable crown, but we for* **an imperishable crown.**

²⁶ *Therefore I run thus:* <u>not with uncertainty</u>. *Thus* <u>I fight: not as one who beats the air</u>. ²⁷ *But* <u>I discipline my body</u> *and* <u>bring it into subjection,</u> *lest, when I have preached to others, I myself should become disqualified. (Emphasis mine)*

Proper stewardship of an instruction involves discipline of the spirit, soul (v. 17), **and body** (v. 26).

Crown of Glory

This crown is given to those who serve faithfully as leaders in the church, particularly pastors or elders, who shepherd God's people with humility and diligence. It's mentioned in 1 Peter 5:4, highlighting the reward for spiritual leadership and care for others.

This crown is given to those who pursue wisdom and understanding.

1 Peter 5:4:

And when the Chief Shepherd appears, you will receive the **crown of glory** *that will never fade away. (Emphasis mine)*

Proverbs 4:7-9:

> *⁷ Wisdom is the principal thing; therefore get wisdom. and in all your getting, get understanding. ⁸ Exalt her, and she will promote you; she will bring you honor, when you embrace her. ⁹ <u>She will place on your head an ornament of grace</u>; a **crown of glory** she will deliver to you. (Emphasis mine)*

Crown of Rejoicing

Often called the "soul winner's crown," this is promised to those who lead others to Christ and bring them into the faith. It's mentioned in 1 Thessalonians 2:19-20, celebrating those who joyfully share the gospel and witness to others. Because we understand the concept of lingering human spirits, the definition of soul-winning takes on a whole new light.[11]

This crown is given to those who see those they have served in the presence of the Lord at the unveiling of Jesus within them.

1 Thessalonians 2:17-20:

> *¹⁷ But we, brethren, having been taken away from you for a short time in presence, not in*

---

[11] See Dr. Horner's books, *Lingering Human Spirits* & *Lingering Human Spirits – Volume 2* (LifeSpring Publishing)

*heart, endeavored more eagerly to see your face with great desire. ¹⁸ Therefore, we wanted to come to you—even I, Paul, time and again—but Satan hindered us. ¹⁹ For what is our hope, or joy, or **crown of rejoicing**? Is it not even <u>you in the presence of our Lord</u> Jesus Christ at His coming (unveiling)? ²⁰ For you are our glory and joy. (Emphasis mine)*

Crown of Righteousness

This crown is awarded to those who long for Christ's appearing and live a righteous life in anticipation of His appearing. It symbolizes a life of faithful devotion and anticipation of Christ's second coming. 2 Timothy 4:8 speaks of this crown.

This crown is given to those who love the appearing of Jesus in His sons. Not speaking of a rapture event.

2 Timothy 4:5-8:

> *⁵ But you be watchful in all things, endure afflictions, do the work of an evangelist, fulfill your ministry.*
>
> *⁶ For I am already being poured out as a drink offering, and the time of my departure is at hand. ⁷ I have fought the good fight, I have finished the race, I have kept the faith. ⁸ Finally, there is laid up for me **the crown of righteousness**, which the Lord, the righteous Judge, will give to me on*

that Day, and <u>not to me only but also to all who have loved His appearing.</u> (Emphasis mine)

Crown of Victory (Victor's Crown)

This is another interpretation based on Paul's description of the Christian life as a race or athletic contest. It emphasizes the victory Christians attain over sin and the world by enduring faithfully. This can be connected to the Imperishable Crown, but it's more specifically about the triumph achieved through Christ's victory over death. In some Christian traditions, this victory crown symbolizes success in spiritual warfare and the conquest over temptation.

This crown is given to those who run the race of the Christian walk with diligence and faithfulness.

1 Corinthians 9:24-25:

> *[24] Do you not know that in a race all the runners run, but only one gets the prize? Run in such a way as to get the prize. [25] Everyone who competes in the games goes into strict training. They do it to get a crown that will not last, but **we do it to get a crown that will last forever.** (NIV) (Emphasis mine)*

Crown of Glory

While more commonly associated with leadership in the church, the broader idea of the Crown of Glory can also be seen as a promise to all believers who live faithful lives, reflecting the glory that God bestows on them in eternity. In the New Testament, some refer to the idea that all believers, in the end, will receive this eternal crown as part of their inheritance in Christ.

This crown is given to the elders who have partaken of the glory that has been revealed.

Revelation 22:12:

Look, I am coming soon! My reward is with me, and I will give to each person according to what they have done.

1 Peter 5:1-14:

¹ The elders who are among you I exhort, I who am a fellow elder and a witness of the sufferings of Christ, and also a partaker of the glory that will be revealed:

*² Shepherd the flock of God which is among you, serving as overseers, not by compulsion but willingly, not for dishonest gain but eagerly; ³ nor as being lords over those entrusted to you, but being examples to the flock; ⁴ and when the Chief Shepherd appears, you will receive **the***

crown of glory *that does not fade away. (Emphasis mine)*

Crown of Glory and Honor

This crown is given to the one who endured suffering and tasted death for everyone.

Psalms 8:5:

For You have made him a little lower than the ~~angels~~ *(Elohim), and You have **crowned him with glory and honor**. (Emphasis mine)*

Also...

Hebrews 2:7

*You have made him a little lower than the angels, And You have **crowned him with glory and honor** and set Him over the works of Your hands. (Emphasis mine)*

And...

Hebrews 2:9-11:

*⁹ But we see Jesus, who was made a little lower than the angels, for the suffering of death **crowned with glory and honor,** that He, by the grace of God, **might taste death for everyone.***

10 For it was fitting for Him, for whom are all things and by whom are all things, in bringing many sons to glory, to make the captain of their salvation perfect through sufferings.

11 For both He who sanctifies and those who are being sanctified are all of one, for which reason He is not ashamed to call them brethren. (Emphasis mine)

Because we are sons, we are not
made lower than the angels.
We embrace a place
of sonship with the Father
with Jesus as our elder brother.

Crown of Justice

This crown is given to those who operate with justice in the Courts of Heaven.

Deuteronomy 33:20-21:

*20 And of Gad he said: 'Blessed is he who enlarges Gad; he dwells as a lion, and tears the arm and **the crown of his head**. 21 He provided the first part for himself, because a lawgiver's portion was reserved there. He came with the heads of the people; **he administered the justice of the***

LORD, and His judgments with Israel.'
(Emphasis mine)

The Father wants the sons to learn to administer justice and judgment according to His design, not our own. Remember, if you do not love someone, you do not deserve to sit in judgment of them, nor should you try to administer justice to them. If your "justice" is not from love, it is not justice and will result in injustice.

Crown of the Aaronic Priesthood

This crown is given to those who serve in the Aaronic Priesthood.

Exodus 29:4-7:

> *[4] And Aaron and his sons you shall bring to the door of the tabernacle of meeting, and you shall wash them with water. [5] Then you shall take the garments, put the tunic on Aaron, and the robe of the ephod, the ephod, and the breastplate, and gird him with the intricately woven band of the ephod. [6] You shall put the turban on his head, and put **the holy crown** on the turban. [7] And you shall take the anointing oil, pour it on his head, and anoint him. (Emphasis mine)*

Crown of Isolation

This crown is given when one is separated from their brothers for the purposes of God.

Genesis 49:25-26:

> *²⁵ By the God of your father who will help you, and by the Almighty who will bless you with blessings of Heaven above, blessings of the deep that lies beneath, blessings of the breasts and of the womb. ²⁶ The blessings of your father have excelled the blessings of my ancestors, up to the utmost bound of the everlasting hills. they shall be on the head of Joseph, and on the **crown of the head of him** who was separate from his brothers. (Emphasis mine)*

Crown of the Spirit of Justice

This crown is given to those who sit in judgment righteously and turn back battles at the gate.

Isaiah 28:5-8:

> *⁵ In that day the LORD of hosts will be for **a crown of glory and a diadem of beauty** to the remnant of His people, ⁶ for <u>a spirit of justice to him who sits in judgment,</u> and <u>for strength to those who turn back the battle at the gate</u>. (Emphasis mine)*

To the Drunkards of Ephraim

⁷ But they also have erred through wine, and through intoxicating drink are out of the way; the priest and the prophet have erred through intoxicating drink, they are swallowed up by wine, they are out of the way through intoxicating drink; they err in vision, they stumble in judgment. ⁸ For all tables are full of vomit and filth; no place is clean.

The Prophets and Priests of Ephraim had allowed their soul and body realms to have dominion. As a result, they forfeited clear vision and sound judgment. You can be drunk with a sense of self-importance, thus making yourself of no positive Kingdom value.

Crown of the Defeat of Your Enemies

This crown is given to the victors in battle.

2 Samuel 12:26-31:

²⁶ Now Joab fought against Rabbah of the people of Ammon, and took the royal city. ²⁷ And Joab sent messengers to David, and said, 'I have fought against Rabbah, and I have taken the city's water supply. ²⁸ Now, therefore, gather the rest of the people together and encamp against the city and take it, lest I take the city and it be called after my name.'

*²⁹ So David gathered all the people together and went to Rabbah, fought against it, and took it. ³⁰ Then **he took their king's crown from his head**. Its weight was a talent[12] of gold, with precious stones. **And it was set on David's head**. Also he brought out the spoil of the city in great abundance. ³¹ And he brought out the people who were in it, and put them to work with saws and iron picks and iron axes, and made them cross over to the brick works. So he did to all the cities of the people of Ammon. Then David and all the people returned to Jerusalem. (Also in 1 Chronicles 20:2) (Emphasis mine)*

To the victor belongs the spoils.

Father not only wants us to be victorious in battle, but also to obtain the spoils of that battle, including the dominion the captured crowns represent.

Crown of Kingship

This crown is given to those who receive stolen inheritances back.

---

[12] A talent was possibly 7 pounds.

Jehoash became king and Athaliah (daughter of Jezebel and Ahab) was killed. Athaliah was one who stole inheritances.

Backstory: After the death of Jezebel and Ahab at the hands of Jehu, Athaliah proclaimed herself queen of Judah. She had all the possible heirs to the throne killed. However, one of her grandsons, Joash, was hidden away in the temple by his aunt Jehosheba and the High Priest Jehoiada for six years. He then staged a coup and brought out Jehoash and crowned him king and had Athaliah killed.

2 Kings 11:9-12:

> *[9] So the captains of the hundreds did according to all that Jehoiada the priest commanded. Each of them took his men who were to be on duty on the Sabbath, with those who were going off duty on the Sabbath, and came to Jehoiada the priest. [10] And the priest gave the captains of hundreds the spears and shields which had belonged to King David, that were in the temple of the LORD.*
>
> *[11] Then the escorts stood, every man with his weapons in his hand, all around the king, from the right side of the temple to the left side of the temple, by the altar and the house. [12] And he brought out the king's son,* **put the crown on him***, and gave him the Testimony; they made him king and anointed him, and they clapped*

their hands and said, 'Long live the king!' (Also 2 Chronicles 23:11) (Emphasis mine)

The Father desires for the rightful heirs to find their place as sons.

Crown of Vashti

This crown was worn by Vashti until her death due to her disobedience to the King.

Disobedience to the King can result in you losing your position of authority and your crown.

Esther 1:10-22:

> *[10] On the seventh day, when the heart of the king was merry with wine, he commanded Mehuman, Biztha, Harbona, Bigtha, Abagtha, Zethar, and Carcas, seven eunuchs who served in the presence of King Ahasuerus, [11] to bring Queen Vashti before the king, wearing her royal crown, in order to show her beauty to the people and the officials, for she was beautiful to behold. [12] But Queen Vashti refused to come at the king's command brought by his eunuchs; therefore the king was furious, and his anger burned within him.*
>
> *[13] Then the king said to the wise men who understood the times (for this was the king's manner toward all who knew law and justice,*

14 those closest to him being Carshena, Shethar, Admatha, Tarshish, Meres, Marsena, and Memucan, the seven princes of Persia and Media, who had access to the king's presence, and who ranked highest in the kingdom): 15 'What shall we do to Queen Vashti, according to law, because she did not obey the command of King Ahasuerus brought to her by the eunuchs?'

16 And Memucan answered before the king and the princes: 'Queen Vashti has <u>not only wronged the king, but also all the princes, and all the people who are in all the provinces of King Ahasuerus.</u> 17 For the queen's behavior will become known to all women, so that they will despise their husbands in their eyes, when they report, 'King Ahasuerus commanded Queen Vashti to be brought in before him, but she did not come.' 18 This very day the noble ladies of Persia and Media will say to all the king's officials that they have heard of the behavior of the queen. Thus there will be excessive contempt and wrath.

19 If it pleases the king, let a royal decree go out from him, and let it be recorded in the laws of the Persians and the Medes, so that it will not be altered, that Vashti shall come no more before King Ahasuerus; and let the king give her royal position to another who is better than she. 20 When the king's decree which he will make is proclaimed throughout all his empire (for it is great), **all wives will honor their husbands, both great and small.'**

²¹ And the reply pleased the king and the princes, and the king did according to the word of Memucan. ²² Then he sent letters to all the king's provinces, to each province in its own script, and to every people in their own language, that each man should be master in his own house, and speak in the language of his own people. (Emphasis mine)

Vashti's actions resulted in a loss of favor, a loss of an audience with the king, and a loss of position before the king.

Crown of Esther

This crown is given to those fully prepared to give themselves to the King.

Esther 2:16-18:

¹⁶ So Esther was taken to King Ahasuerus, into his royal palace, in the tenth month, which is the month of Tebeth, in the seventh year of his reign. ¹⁷ The king loved Esther more than all the other women, and she **obtained grace and favor in his sight more than all the virgins; so he set the royal crown upon her head and made her queen instead of Vashti.** *¹⁸ Then the king* *made a great feast, the Feast of Esther, for all his officials and servants; and he proclaimed a holiday in the provinces and gave gifts according to the generosity of a king. (Emphasis mine)*

Simple obedience and submission to the King in the times of waiting will result in the elevation by the King when the preparation time is over.

- She experienced favor to be selected as a candidate for queen.
- She experienced favor in her times of preparation.
- She walked with humility and wisdom before her presentation to the King.
- She obtained favor from the King and became queen.

Esther went from orphan to queen in approximately one year. Much can be learned from her story, especially concerning preparation for wearing a crown. That could be its own book.

———— ∞ ————

Chapter 10
Types of Crowns in Scripture
Part 2

Crown of Favor/Honor

The crown of favor/honor is given to those who the King (God) favors.

Esther 8:15-17:

> ¹⁵ *So Mordecai went out from the presence of the king in royal apparel of blue and white,* **with a great crown of gold and a garment of fine linen and purple;** *and the city of Shushan rejoiced and was glad.* ¹⁶ **The Jews had light and gladness, joy and honor.** ¹⁷ *And in every province and city, wherever the king's command and decree came, the Jews had joy and gladness, a feast and a holiday. Then many of the people of the land became Jews, because fear of the Jews fell upon them. (Emphasis mine)*

The favor of God will extend to your broader audience.

Crown of David

This crown is given to those with the heart of David.

Psalms 89:20-52:

> [20] I have found My servant David; With My holy oil I have anointed him, [21] with whom My hand shall be established; also My arm shall strengthen him.
>
> [22] The enemy shall not outwit him, nor the son of wickedness afflict him.
>
> [23] I will beat down his foes before his face, and plague those who hate him. [24] 'But My faithfulness and My mercy shall be with him, and in My name his horn shall be exalted. [25] Also I will set his hand over the sea, and his right hand over the rivers.
>
> [26] He shall cry to Me, 'You are my Father, My God, and the rock of my salvation.'
>
> [27] Also <u>I will make him My firstborn</u>, the highest of the kings of the earth. [28] My mercy I will keep for him forever, and My covenant shall stand firm with him. [29] His seed also I will make to endure forever, and his throne as the days of heaven. *(Emphasis mine)*

If His sons mess up, then...

30 'If his sons forsake My law And do not walk in My judgments, 31 If they break My statutes And do not keep My commandments, 32 then <u>I will punish their transgression with the rod, and their iniquity with stripes</u>.

*33 **Nevertheless** My lovingkindness I will not utterly take from him, Nor allow My faithfulness to fail. 34 <u>My covenant I will not break, nor alter the word that has gone out of My lips</u>.*

35 Once I have sworn by My holiness; I will not lie to David: 36 <u>His seed shall endure forever, and his throne as the sun before Me</u>; 37 It shall be established forever like the moon, Even like the faithful witness in the sky.' Selah (Emphasis mine)

The Result of Dishonor

38 But You have cast off and abhorred, You have been furious with Your anointed.

39 You have renounced the covenant of Your servant; You have profaned his crown by casting it to the ground.

40 You have broken down all his hedges; You have brought his strongholds to ruin. 41 All who pass by the way plunder him; He is a reproach to his neighbors.

⁴² *You have exalted the right hand of his adversaries; You have made all his enemies rejoice.*

⁴³ *You have also turned back the edge of his sword, and have not sustained him in the battle.*

⁴⁴ *You have made his glory cease, and cast his throne down to the ground.*

⁴⁵ *The days of his youth You have shortened; You have covered him with shame. Selah*

The Plea for Mercy

⁴⁶ *How long, LORD? Will You hide Yourself forever? Will Your wrath burn like fire?*

⁴⁷ *Remember how short my time is; for what futility have You created all the children of men?*

⁴⁸ *What man can live and not see death? Can he deliver his life from the power of the grave? Selah*

⁴⁹ *Lord, where are Your former lovingkindnesses, which You swore to David in Your truth?*

⁵⁰ *Remember, Lord, the reproach of Your servants how I bear in my bosom the reproach of all the many peoples, ⁵¹ with which Your enemies have reproached, O LORD, with which they have reproached the footsteps of Your anointed.*

⁵² Blessed be the LORD forevermore! Amen, and amen. (Emphasis mine)

A crown can be profaned
by being cast to the ground.

If a crown has been profaned, repentance is required.

Results of Dishonor on the One Guilty of Dishonoring:

- You lose your position and impact your reputation due to your anger toward the target of your dishonor.

³⁸ But You have cast off and abhorred, You have been furious with Your anointed.

³⁹ You have renounced the covenant of Your servant; You have profaned his crown by casting it to the ground.

- Where you may have previously been in covenant relationship with someone, that relationship is now broken. You have profaned his crown by your dishonor.

⁴⁰ You have broken down all his hedges; You have brought his strongholds to ruin. ⁴¹ All who pass by the way plunder him; He is a reproach to his neighbors.

You have created breaches that will impact his life. Your dishonor impacts the things the person has done to build for the Kingdom. Your disdain causes others to see him in a negative light.

> [42] *You have exalted the right hand of his adversaries; You have made all his enemies rejoice.*

- You have cooperated with the enemy and done their dirty work for them. Your enemies are happy for the help. You made their job easier.

> [43] *You have also turned back the edge of his sword, and have not sustained him in the battle.*

You have impacted his ability to war effectively, and you have not stood up for him in battle. You have betrayed him.

The negative impacts of dishonor cannot be ignored. I have been the victim of dishonor, and I can say unequivocally that it is not pleasant, nor does it honor the Lord.

Heaven taught us years ago about governing the whispers because most dishonor occurs when people fail to govern and shut down the whispers of accusations and false verdicts over others' lives, and those whispers eventually become a shout! Unresolved whispers often result in offenses that should have no place in our spiritual house.

Crown of Flourishing

This crown is given to those who worship with abandon and have the Lord as their resting place.

Psalms 132:17-18:

> *^{17} There I will make the horn of David grow; I will prepare a lamp for My Anointed.*
>
> *^{18} His enemies I will clothe with shame, but upon Himself **His crown** shall flourish. (Emphasis mine)*

Crown of Longevity

This crown is given to those who have asked life of the Father.

Psalms 21:1-6:

> *^{1} The king (David) shall have joy in Your strength, O LORD; and in Your salvation how greatly shall he rejoice! ^{2} You have given him his heart's desire, and have not withheld the request of his lips. Selah*
>
> *^{3} For You meet him with the blessings of goodness; You set **a crown of pure gold** upon his head. ^{4} <u>He asked life from You, and You gave it to him—length of days forever and ever</u>. ^{5} His glory is great in Your salvation; <u>honor and majesty</u> You have placed upon him. ^{6} For You*

have made him most blessed forever; You have made him exceedingly glad with Your presence. (Emphasis mine)

Crown of the Wise

This crown is given to those who have pursued wisdom.

Proverbs 14:24:

> **The crown of the wise** *is their riches, But the foolishness of fools is folly. (Emphasis mine)*

Their riches are the wisdom they possess.

The Crown of the Godly Wife

This crown describes the godly wife.

Proverbs 12:4:

> *An excellent wife is* **the crown of her husband***, but she who causes shame is like rottenness in his bones. (Emphasis mine)*

Crown of the Old Man

This crown is given to those fathers who have fathered well.

Proverbs 17:6:

*Children's children are **the crown of old men**,*
And the glory of children is their father.
(Emphasis mine)

Each generation
must pursue crowns

Proverbs 27:24:

*For riches are not forever, **nor does a crown endure to all generations**. (Emphasis mine)*

Crown of Royalty

This crown is given to those who were once outcasts but are now favored by the Lord.

Ezekiel 16:8-14:

> [8] 'When I passed by you again and looked upon you, indeed your time was the time of love; so I spread My wing over you and covered your nakedness. Yes, I swore an oath to you and entered into a covenant with you, and you became Mine,' says the Lord GOD.
>
> [9] 'Then I washed you in water; yes, I thoroughly washed off your blood, and I anointed you with oil. [10] I clothed you in embroidered cloth and gave you sandals of badger skin; I clothed you with fine linen and covered you with silk. [11] I

*adorned you with ornaments, put bracelets on your wrists, and a chain on your neck. ¹² And I put a jewel in your nose, earrings in your ears, and **a beautiful crown on your head**.*

¹³ Thus you were adorned with gold and silver, and your clothing was of fine linen, silk, and embroidered cloth. You ate pastry of fine flour, honey, and oil. You were exceedingly beautiful, and succeeded to royalty. ¹⁴ Your fame went out among the nations because of your beauty, for it was perfect through My splendor which I had bestowed on you,' says the Lord GOD. (Emphasis mine)

Crown of the Branch/
Crown of Memorial/Elaborate Crown

This crown was given to Joshua the High Priest for faithful stewardship.

This will be discussed in the chapter on the Royal Priesthood of the Crown.

Crown of the Conqueror

This crown is given to the conquering ones.

Revelation 6:1-2:

¹ Now I saw when the Lamb opened one of the seals, and I heard one of the four living creatures saying with a voice like thunder, 'Come and see.'

*² And I looked, and behold, a white horse. He who sat on it had a bow, and **a crown was given to him**, and he went out conquering and to conquer. (Emphasis mine)*

Crown of the King of Kings

This crown is given to Jesus.

Revelation 14:14:

*Then I looked, and behold, a white cloud, and on the cloud sat One like the Son of Man, having on His head a **golden crown**, and in His hand a sharp sickle. (Emphasis mine)*

Crown of Knowledge

This crown is given to those who pursue knowledge via the Tree of Life.

Proverbs 14:18:

*The simple inherit folly, But the prudent are **crowned with knowledge**. (Emphasis mine)*

Crown of Endurance

This crown is given to those who compete according to the rules.

2 Timothy 2:1-10:

¹ You therefore, my son, be strong in the grace that is in Christ Jesus. ² And the things that you have heard from me among many witnesses, commit these to faithful men who will be able to teach others also.

³ You therefore must endure hardship as a good soldier of Jesus Christ. ⁴ No one engaged in warfare entangles himself with the affairs of this life, that he may please him who enlisted him as a soldier. ⁵ And also if anyone competes in athletics, he is not <u>crowned unless he competes according to the rules</u>.

⁶ The hardworking farmer must be first to partake of the crops. ⁷ Consider what I say, and may the Lord give you understanding in all things.

⁸ Remember that Jesus Christ, of the seed of David, was raised from the dead according to my gospel, ⁹ for which I suffer trouble as an evildoer, even to the point of chains; but the word of God is not chained.

¹⁰ Therefore I endure all things for the sake of the elect, that they also may obtain the salvation which is in Christ Jesus with eternal glory. (Emphasis mine)

You can disqualify yourself from receiving a crown by not competing according to the rules.

Crown of Lovingkindness and Tender Mercies

This crown is given to those whose heart is after the Lord.

Psalms 103:1-22:

His Lovingkindness

¹ A Psalm Of David. Bless the LORD, O my soul; and all that is within me, bless His holy name!

² Bless the LORD, O my soul, and forget not all His benefits: ³ Who forgives all your iniquities, who heals all your diseases, ⁴ who redeems your life from destruction, who crowns you with lovingkindness and tender mercies, ⁵ who satisfies your mouth with good things, so that your youth is renewed like the eagle's.

His Tender Mercies

⁶ The LORD executes righteousness and justice for all who are oppressed. ⁷ He made known His ways to Moses, His acts to the children of Israel. ⁸ <u>The LORD is merciful</u> and gracious, slow to anger, and <u>abounding in mercy</u>.

⁹ He will not always strive with us, nor will He keep His anger forever. ¹⁰ He has not dealt with us according to <u>our sins</u>, nor punished us according to <u>our iniquities</u>. ¹¹ For as the heavens are high above the earth, so great is <u>His mercy</u> toward those who fear Him; ¹² As far as the east is from the west, so far has He removed <u>our transgressions</u> from us.

¹³ As a father pities his children, so the LORD pities those who fear Him. ¹⁴ For He knows our frame; He remembers that we are dust.

¹⁵ As for man, his days are like grass; as a flower of the field, so he flourishes.

¹⁶ For the wind passes over it, and it is gone, and its place remembers it no more.

¹⁷ But <u>the mercy of the LORD</u> is from everlasting to everlasting on those who fear Him, and His righteousness to children's children,

¹⁸ To such as keep His covenant, and to those who remember His commandments to do them.

¹⁹ The LORD has established His throne in Heaven, And His kingdom rules over all.

²⁰ Bless the LORD, you His angels, who excel in strength, who do His word, heeding the voice of His Word.

²¹ Bless the LORD, all you His hosts, you ministers of His, who do His pleasure.

²² Bless the LORD, all His works, in all places of His dominion. Bless the LORD, O my soul! (Emphasis mine)

As mentioned early in this book, the prophetic word we received was:

The restoration of crowns is just the beginning.

Many have lost territories that need to be restored.

Others have lost inheritances that need restoration.

Now that they have gone in and reclaimed their crowns have them step into the Court of Crowns and receive **renewed authorization for the authority that had been lost**.

Explore this Court for it is part of the retaking of lands and properties, gold, and treasure, all of which have been waiting for the sons to step into a new level of sonship in this day and hour.

That which has stolen needs to be reclaimed and that done seven-fold.

How to determine what crowns have been lost or stolen:

- Visit the Court of Crowns and ask to see the records for you
- Pray in the Spirit and request understanding to come.
- Request Access to the Court of Crowns
- Repent for your part in the loss or forfeiture
- Request the restoration of the crown
- Request the restoration of the authority and dominion of that crown in your life.
- **Then, commission the angels to begin bringing in what has been lost and fill the capacity.** That capacity can also be enlarged.
- Rejoice!

---

*Use your authority
to call in the treasure.*

———— ∞ ————

Chapter 11
Types of Crowns in Scripture
Part 3

Crown of the Wedding Day

This crown was placed upon Solomon's head at his wedding by Bathsheba.

Song of Solomon 3:11:

> *Go forth, O daughters of Zion, And see King Solomon with **the crown** with which his mother **crowned** him on the day of his wedding, The day of the gladness of his heart. (Emphasis mine)*

Tyre was known as the crowning city

Isaiah 23:8-9:

*⁸ Who has taken this counsel against **Tyre, the crowning city**, whose merchants are princes, Whose traders are the honorable of the earth?*

⁹ The LORD of hosts has purposed it, to bring to dishonor the pride of all glory, to bring into contempt all the honorable of the earth. (Emphasis mine)

Cities can have a crowning glory!

That crowning glory
can be forfeited due to pride.

Crown of Thorns

This crown was worn by Jesus before His crucifixion.

Matthew 27:27-31:

²⁷ Then the soldiers of the governor took Jesus into the Praetorium and gathered the whole garrison around Him. ²⁸ And they stripped Him and put a scarlet robe on Him. ²⁹ When they had twisted a crown of thorns, they put it on His head, and a reed (symbolic of a scepter) in His right hand. And they bowed the knee before Him and mocked Him, saying, 'Hail, King of the Jews!'

30 Then they spat on Him, and took the reed and struck Him on the head. 31 And when they had mocked Him, they took the robe off Him, put His own clothes on Him, and led Him away to be crucified.

John 19:1-12:

1So then Pilate took Jesus and scourged Him.

*2 And the soldiers twisted **a crown of thorns and put it on His head**, and they put on Him <u>a purple robe</u>.*

3 Then they said, 'Hail, King of the Jews!' And they struck Him with their hands.

4 Pilate then went out again and said to them, "Behold, I am bringing Him out to you, that you may know that I find no fault in Him."

*5 Then Jesus came out, wearing **the crown of thorns** and <u>the purple robe</u>. And Pilate said to them, 'Behold the Man!'*

6 Therefore, when the chief priests and officers saw Him, they cried out, saying, 'Crucify Him, crucify Him!' Pilate said to them, 'You take Him and crucify Him, for I find no fault in Him.'

7 The Jews answered him, 'We have a law, and according to our law, he ought to die because He made Himself the Son of God.'

⁸ Therefore, when Pilate heard that saying, he was the more afraid, ⁹ and went again into the Praetorium, and said to Jesus, 'Where are You from?' But Jesus gave him no answer.

¹⁰ Then Pilate said to Him, 'Are you not speaking to me? Do You not know that I have power to crucify you, and power to release You?'

¹¹ Jesus answered, 'You could have no power at all against me unless it had been given you from above. Therefore the one who delivered me to you has the greater sin.'

¹² From then on Pilate sought to release him, but the Jews cried out, saying, 'If you let this man go, you are not Caesar's friend. Whoever makes himself a king speaks against Caesar.' (Emphasis mine)

The soldiers' mockery of Jesus did not negate the authority He carried.

---

¹¹ You could have no power at all against Me unless it had been given you from above.

Principle: The Father can give permission for certain things to happen in your life.

Crown of Goodness for the Year

This crown is given to those whose actions please the Lord.

Psalms 65:1-13:

¹ Praise is awaiting You, O God, in Zion; and to You the vow shall be performed. ² O You who hear prayer, to You all flesh will come. ³ Iniquities prevail against me; as for our transgressions, you will provide atonement for them.

⁴ Blessed is the man You choose, and cause to approach You, that he may dwell in Your courts. We shall be satisfied with the goodness of Your house, of Your holy temple. ⁵ By awesome deeds in righteousness You will answer us, O God of our salvation, You who are the confidence of all the ends of the earth, and of the far-off seas; ⁶ who established the mountains by His strength, being clothed with power; ⁷ You who still the noise of the seas, the noise of their waves, and the tumult of the peoples. ⁸ They also who dwell in the farthest parts are afraid of Your signs; You make the outgoings of the morning and evening rejoice.

⁹ You visit the earth and water it, You greatly enrich it; the river of God is full of water; You provide their grain, for so You have prepared it.

¹⁰ You water its ridges abundantly, You settle its furrows; You make it soft with showers, You bless its growth.

*¹¹ You **crown the year** with Your goodness, and Your paths drip with abundance.*

¹² They drop on the pastures of the wilderness, and the little hills rejoice on every side.

¹³ The pastures are clothed with flocks; the valleys also are covered with grain; they shout for joy, they also sing. (Emphasis mine)

Elders Crowns

This crown was given to the 24 Elders.

Revelation 4:4:

*Around the throne were twenty-four thrones, and on the thrones I saw twenty-four elders sitting, clothed in white robes; and they had **crowns of gold** on their heads. (Emphasis mine)*

Revelation 4:10-11:

*¹⁰ ...the twenty-four elders fall down before Him who sits on the throne and worship Him who lives forever and ever, and **cast their crowns before the throne**, saying: ¹¹ 'You are worthy, O Lord, to receive glory and honor and power; for*

You created all things, and by Your will they exist and were created.' (Emphasis mine)

Revelation 13:9-10:

*⁹ If anyone has an ear, let him hear. ¹⁰ **He who leads into captivity shall go into captivity; he who kills with the sword must be killed** with the sword. Here is the patience and the faith of the saints.*

Revelation 19:11-16:

*¹¹ Now I saw Heaven opened, and behold, a white horse. And He who sat on him was called Faithful and True, and in righteousness He judges and makes war. ¹² His eyes were like **a flame of fire**, and on His head were **many crowns**. He had a name written that no one knew except Himself. ¹³ He was clothed with a robe dipped in blood, and His name is called the Word of God. ¹⁴ And the armies in heaven, clothed in fine linen, white and clean, followed Him on white horses.*

¹⁵ Now out of His mouth goes a sharp sword, that with it He should strike the nations. And He Himself will rule them with a rod of iron. He Himself treads the winepress of the fierceness and wrath of Almighty God. ¹⁶ And He has on His robe and on His thigh a name written: king of Kings and Lord of lords.

> *Remember:*
> *To de-crown you is to de-throne you.*

In scripture, we see that crowns were created for kings, queens, princes, and priests. Heaven has quite the variety.

The Crown of Contempt

This crown is given to those going through desolate places.

Job 31:34-40:

> *[34] Because I feared the great multitude, And dreaded **the contempt of families**, so that I kept silence and did not go out of the door— [35] Oh, that I had one to hear me! Here is my mark. Oh, that the Almighty would answer me, that my prosecutor had written a book!*
>
> *[36] Surely I would carry it on my shoulder, and bind it on me **like a crown**; [37] I would declare to Him the number of my steps; like a prince I would approach Him.*
>
> *[38] 'If my land cries out against me, and its furrows weep together; [39] If I have eaten its fruit without money, or caused its owners to lose their lives; [40] then let thistles grow instead of*

wheat, and weeds instead of barley.' The words of Job are ended. (Emphasis mine)

This may be a crown you don't want to seek after, but it rewards those who find themselves in desolate and lonely places.

———— ∞ ————

Chapter 12

Undesirable Crowns

Scripture describes several crowns that we should not seek to obtain. Some are the result of lifestyles, while nearly ALL of them are the result of bad decisions. We are all faced with wrong voices, which often results in wrong choices being made. Heaven is trying to free us from all of that, and sometimes, it is helpful to see contributing factors to things you don't want operating in your life. Understand that these inferior crowns still have a degree of authority. For example, the first crown listed, the Crown of the Wicked, is not granted by Heaven but by hell and is bestowed on those given over to wickedness. It will also empower more wickedness to manifest in the wearer's lives. It is the same with the other undesirable crowns listed.

An interesting thing to note that, when removing an ungodly crown, the person often feels as if they have been poked in their scalp. The sense is that the ungodly crowns are often inverted when placed upon a person, giving the sensation of being poked or stabbed.

Crown of the Wicked

This crown is given to those given to wickedness.

Ezekiel 23:42:

*The sound of a carefree multitude was with her, and Sabeans were brought from the wilderness with men of the common sort, who put <u>bracelets on their wrists</u> and **beautiful crowns** on their heads. (Emphasis mine)*

The wicked can crown you according to their desires. They may have a type of beauty, but not one given by God.

Crown of Torment

This crown is given worn by the locust afflicting mankind in Revelation 9. It is not worn by humans, but hybrids.

Revelation 9:3-10:

[3] Then out of the smoke locusts came upon the earth. And to them was given power, as the scorpions of the earth have power. [4] They were commanded not to harm the grass of the earth, or any green thing, or any tree, but only those

men who do not have the seal of God on their foreheads. ⁵ And they were not given authority to kill them, but to torment them for five months. Their torment was like the torment of a scorpion when it strikes a man.

⁶ In those days men will seek death and will not find it; they will desire to die, and death will flee from them. ⁷ The shape of the locusts was like horses prepared for battle. On their heads were **crowns of something like gold**, *and their faces were like the faces of men. ⁸ They had hair like women's hair, and their teeth were like lions' teeth. ⁹ And they had breastplates like breastplates of iron, and the sound of their wings was like the sound of chariots with many horses running into battle. ¹⁰ They had tails like scorpions, and there were stings in their tails. Their power was to hurt men five months. (Emphasis mine)*

v. 7 The crowns represented the authority these locusts carried to afflict men for five months.

Crown of the Beast

This crown is worn by the Beast of Revelation 13.

Revelation 13:1-10:

¹ Then I stood on the sand of the sea. And I saw a beast rising up out of the sea, having seven heads and ten horns, and on his horns **ten crowns**, and on his heads a blasphemous name.

² Now the beast which I saw was like a leopard, his feet were like the feet of a bear, and his mouth like the mouth of a lion. The dragon gave him his power, his throne, and great authority. ³ And I saw one of his heads as if it had been mortally wounded, and his deadly wound was healed. And all the world marveled and followed the beast.

⁴ So they worshiped the dragon who gave authority to the beast; and they worshiped the beast, saying, 'Who is like the beast? Who is able to make war with him?' ⁵ And he was given a mouth speaking great things and blasphemies, and he was given authority to continue for forty-two months.

⁶ Then he opened his mouth in blasphemy against God, to blaspheme His name, His tabernacle, and those who dwell in heaven.⁷ It was granted to him to make war with the saints and to overcome them. And authority was given him over every tribe, tongue, and nation.⁸ All who dwell on the earth will worship him, whose names have not been written in the Book of Life of the Lamb slain from the foundation of the world. (Emphasis mine)

Crown of Adultery

This crown is given to those given over to sexual promiscuity.

Jeremiah 13:15-27:

> *15 Hear and give ear: Do not be proud, for the LORD has spoken. 16 Give glory to the LORD your God before He causes darkness, and before your feet stumble On the dark mountains, and while you are looking for light, He turns it into the shadow of death and makes it dense darkness. 17 But if you will not hear it, my soul will weep in secret for your pride; my eyes will weep bitterly and run down with tears, because the LORD's flock has been taken captive.*
>
> *18 Say to the king and to the queen mother, 'Humble yourselves; sit down, for your rule shall collapse,* **the crown of your glory**.*' 19 The cities of the South shall be shut up, and no one shall open them; Judah shall be carried away captive, all of it; it shall be wholly carried away captive.*
>
> *20 Lift up your eyes and see those who come from the north. Where is the flock that was given to you, your beautiful sheep? 21 What will you say when He punishes you? For you have taught them to be chieftains, to be head over you. Will not pangs seize you, like a woman in labor? 22 And if you say in your heart, 'Why have these*

things come upon me?' For the greatness of your iniquity your skirts have been uncovered, your heels made bare. ²³ Can the Ethiopian change his skin or the leopard its spots? Then may you also do good who are accustomed to do evil.

²⁴ 'Therefore, I will scatter them like stubble that passes away by the wind of the wilderness.

²⁵ This is your lot, the portion of your measures from Me," says the LORD, 'Because you have forgotten Me and trusted in falsehood. ²⁶ Therefore I will uncover your skirts over your face, that your shame may appear. ²⁷ I have seen your adulteries and your lustful neighings, the lewdness of your harlotry, your abominations on the hills in the fields. Woe to you, O Jerusalem! Will you still not be made clean?' (Emphasis mine)

Crown of Pride

This crown is given to those given over to pride and drunkenness.

Isaiah 28:1-8:

*¹ Woe to the **crown of pride**, to the drunkards of Ephraim, whose glorious beauty is a fading flower which is at the head of the verdant valleys, to those who are overcome with wine!*

² Behold, the Lord has a mighty and strong one, like a tempest of hail and a destroying storm, like a flood of mighty waters overflowing, who will bring them down to the earth with His hand.

*³ **The crown of pride**, the drunkards of Ephraim, **will be trampled underfoot;** ⁴ and the glorious beauty is a fading flower which is at the head of the verdant valley, like the first fruit before the summer, which an observer sees; He eats it up while it is still in his hand. (Emphasis mine)*

Crown of Destruction

The Amalekite who killed Saul died by the words of his mouth when he touched the Lord's anointed. He touched the Crown of Saul.

2 Samuel 1:6-16:

⁶ Then the young man who told him said, 'As I happened by chance to be on Mount Gilboa, there was Saul, leaning on his spear; and indeed the chariots and horsemen followed hard after him.

⁷ 'Now when he looked behind him, he saw me and called to me. And I answered, 'Here I am.' ⁸ And he said to me, 'Who are you?' So I answered him, 'I am an Amalekite.'

⁹ He said to me again, 'Please stand over me and kill me, for anguish has come upon me, but my life still remains in me.'

¹⁰ So I stood over him and killed him, because I was sure that he could not live after he had fallen. And I took **the crown** *that was on his head and* **the bracelet that was on his arm***, and have brought them here to my lord.'*

¹¹ Therefore David took hold of his own clothes and tore them, and so did all the men who were with him. ¹² And they mourned and wept and fasted until evening for Saul and for Jonathan, his son, for the people of the LORD and for the house of Israel, because they had fallen by the sword.

¹³ Then David said to the young man who told him, "Where are you from?" And he answered, 'I am the son of an alien, an Amalekite.' ¹⁴ So David said to him, "How was it you were not afraid to put forth your hand to destroy the LORD's anointed?"

¹⁵ Then David called one of the young men and said, 'Go near, and execute him!' And he struck him so that he died. ¹⁶ So David said to him, 'Your blood is on your own head, for your own mouth has testified against you, saying, 'I have killed the LORD's anointed.' (Emphasis mine)

Touching the Lord's anointed can result in your own destruction. Your mouth may testify against you.

Crown of Tumult

Jeremiah 48:40-47:

> *⁴⁰ For thus says the LORD: 'Behold, one shall fly like an eagle, and spread his wings over Moab. ⁴¹ Kerioth is taken, and the strongholds are surprised; the mighty men's hearts in Moab on that day shall be like the heart of a woman in birth pangs. ⁴² And Moab shall be destroyed as a people because he exalted himself against the LORD. ⁴³ Fear and the pit and the snare shall be upon you, O inhabitant of Moab,' says the LORD.*

> *⁴⁴ 'He who flees from the fear shall fall into the pit, and he who gets out of the pit shall be caught in the snare. For upon Moab, upon it I will bring the year of their punishment,' says the LORD.*

> *⁴⁵ 'Those who fled stood under the shadow of Heshbon Because of exhaustion. But a fire shall come out of Heshbon, a flame from the midst of Sihon, and shall devour the brow of Moab, the **crown of the head of the sons of tumult.***

> *⁴⁶ Woe to you, O Moab! The people of Chemosh perish; for your sons have been taken captive, and your daughters captive.*

⁴⁷ *'Yet I will bring back the captives of Moab In the latter days,' says the LORD. Thus far is the judgment of Moab. (Emphasis mine)*

Crown of Woe

This crown is worn by those who feel forsaken by God.

Job 19:9:

*He has stripped me of my glory, and **taken the crown from my head**. (Emphasis mine)*

Some crowns may be perceived to have been removed by God Himself.

Crown of Idolatry

Jeremiah 2:9-24:

⁹ 'Therefore, I will yet bring charges against you,' says the LORD, 'And against your children's children I will bring charges. ¹⁰ For pass beyond the coasts of Cyprus and see, Send to Kedar and consider diligently, and see if there has been such a thing. ¹¹ Has a nation changed its gods, which are not gods? But My people have changed their Glory for what does not profit. ¹² Be astonished, O heavens, at this, and be horribly afraid; be very desolate," says the

LORD. *¹³ 'For My people have committed two evils: they have forsaken Me, the fountain of living waters, and hewn themselves cisterns— broken cisterns that can hold no water.*

¹⁴ 'Is Israel a servant? Is he a homeborn slave? Why is he plundered? ¹⁵ The young lions roared at him, and growled; they made his land waste; his cities are burned, without inhabitant. ¹⁶ Also the people of Noph and Tahpanhes have **broken the crown** *of your head.*

¹⁷ **Have you not brought this on yourself, in that you have forsaken the LORD your God when He led you in the way?** *¹⁸ And now why take the road to Egypt, to drink the waters of Sihor? Or why take the road to Assyria, to drink the waters of the River? ¹⁹ Your own wickedness will correct you, and your backslidings will rebuke you. Know therefore and see that it is an evil and bitter thing that you have forsaken the LORD your God, and the fear of Me is not in you,' says the Lord GOD of hosts.*

²⁰ 'For of old I have broken your yoke and burst your bonds; and you said, "I will not transgress," when on every high hill and under every green tree you lay down, playing the harlot. ²¹ Yet I had planted you a noble vine, a seed of highest quality. How then have you turned before Me Into the degenerate plant of an alien vine? ²² For though you wash yourself with lye, and use much soap, yet your iniquity is marked before Me,' says the Lord GOD.

²³ 'How can you say, 'I am not polluted, I have not gone after the Baals?' See your way in the valley; know what you have done: you are a swift dromedary breaking loose in her ways, ²⁴ a wild donkey used to the wilderness, that sniffs at the wind in her desire; in her time of mating, who can turn her away? All those who seek her will not weary themselves; in her month they will find her.' (Emphasis mine)

v. 16 People can break the crown of your head.

v. 17 Own your sin. You have forsaken the Lord and the fear of the Lord.

Crown of Wickedness

This crown is given to those who pursue wickedness.

Psalms 7:8-17:

⁸ The LORD shall judge the peoples; judge me, O LORD, according to my righteousness, and according to my integrity within me. ⁹ Oh, let the wickedness of the wicked come to an end, But establish the just; for the righteous God tests the hearts and minds. ¹⁰ My defense is of God, who saves the upright in heart.

¹¹ God is a just judge, and God is angry with the wicked every day. ¹² If he does not turn back, He will sharpen His sword; He bends His bow and makes it ready. ¹³ He also prepares for Himself instruments of death; He makes His arrows into fiery shafts.

*¹⁴ Behold, the wicked brings forth iniquity; yes, he conceives trouble and brings forth falsehood. ¹⁵ He made a pit and dug it out, and has fallen into the ditch which he made. ¹⁶ His trouble shall return upon his own head, And his violent dealing shall come down on **his own crown.***

¹⁷ I will praise the LORD according to His righteousness, and will sing praise to the name of the LORD Most High. (Emphasis mine)

Crown of Desolation

This crown is given to those who are consumed with carnal pleasures.

Isaiah 3:16-26:

¹⁶ Moreover the LORD says: 'Because the daughters of Zion are haughty, and walk with outstretched necks and wanton eyes, walking and mincing as they go, making a jingling with their feet,

*17 Therefore the Lord will strike with a scab **the crown of the head** of the daughters of Zion, and the LORD will uncover their secret parts.'*

18 In that day the Lord will take away the finery: the jingling anklets, the scarves, and the crescents; 19 the pendants, the bracelets, and the veils; 20 the headdresses, the leg ornaments, and the headbands; the perfume boxes, the charms, 21 and the rings; the nose jewels, 22 the festal apparel, and the mantles; the outer garments, the purses, 23 and the mirrors; the fine linen, the turbans, and the robes. 24 And so it shall be: instead of a sweet smell there will be a stench; instead of a sash, a rope; instead of well-set hair, baldness; instead of a rich robe, a girding of sackcloth; and branding instead of beauty.

25 Your men shall fall by the sword, and your mighty in the war. 26 Her gates shall lament and mourn, and she being desolate shall sit on the ground. (Emphasis mine)

Crown of Inheritance

Ezekiel 21:24-26:

24 Therefore, thus says the Lord GOD: 'Because you have made your iniquity to be remembered, in that your transgressions are uncovered, so that in all your doings your sins appear—

because you have come to remembrance, you shall be taken in hand.

*²⁵ Now to you, O profane, wicked prince of Israel, whose day has come, whose iniquity shall end, ²⁶ thus says the Lord GOD: 'Remove the turban, and **take off the crown**; nothing shall remain the same. Exalt the humble, and humble the exalted.' (Emphasis mine)*

Crowns can be lost
because of iniquity.

Perishable Crown

This crown is given to those who preach the Gospel for the wrong reasons.

1 Corinthians 9:16-27:

¹⁶ For if I preach the gospel, I have nothing to boast of, for necessity is laid upon me; yes, woe is me if I do not preach the gospel!

¹⁷ For if I do this willingly, I have a reward; but if against my will, I have been entrusted with a stewardship. ¹⁸ What is my reward then? That when I preach the gospel, I may present the gospel of Christ without charge, that I may <u>not abuse my authority in the gospel</u>.

¹⁹ For though I am free from all men, <u>I have made myself a servant to all, that I might win the more</u>; ²⁰ and to the Jews I became as a Jew, that I might win Jews; to those who are under the law, as under the law, that I might win those who are under the law; ²¹ to those who are without law, as without law (not being without law toward God, but under law toward Christ), that I might win those who are without law; ²² to the weak I became as weak, that I might win the weak. I have become all things to all men, that I might by all means save some.

*²³ Now this I do for the gospel's sake, that I may be partaker of it with you. ²⁴ Do you not know that those who run in a race all run, but one receives the prize? Run in such a way that you may obtain it. ²⁵ And everyone who competes for the prize is temperate in all things. Now they do it to obtain a **perishable crown**, but we for **an imperishable crown**.*

²⁶ Therefore I run thus: not with uncertainty. Thus I fight: not as one who beats the air.

²⁷ But I discipline my body and bring it into subjection, lest, when I have preached to others, I myself should become disqualified. (Emphasis mine)

Philippians 4:1:

*Therefore, my beloved and longed-for brethren, **my joy and crown**, so stand fast in the Lord, beloved. (Emphasis mine)*

Other believers can be your crown

———— ∞ ————

Chapter 13

Crowns Not Listed in Scripture

Although we found many crowns listed in scripture, that is by no means an exhaustive list. Our Bible is only a partial record of the Kingdom-related occurrences that could be written. Remember the Words in the last chapter of John, which state that if the works of Jesus had all been recorded, the world could not contain them. We have already discussed the Crown of Crowns, the Crown of Sonship, the Crown of Everlasting, and the Crown of Discernment. Many other crowns have been made known to us.

- Family Crown – Families have crowns in addition to the Family Crown. These family crowns represent what a family line is to carry into the Earth and manifest for the Kingdom, as well as some other crowns we will talk about in this book.
- Crown of Friendship – Given to those who prove themselves to be true friends. Jesus is the friend

that sticks closer than a brother. Proverbs 18:24: *A man who has friends must himself be friendly, but there is a friend who sticks closer than a brother.*

- Crown of Strength
- Crown of Innocence
- Crown of Provision
- Crown of Stewardship
- Family Crown
- Crown of Legitimacy – Heaven's validation for your work and/or ministry. It may need restoration if others have tried to steal your anointing, ministry, or business.
- Crown of Transition
- Crown of Nurture
- Crown of Parental Love
- Crown of Undoneness
- Crown of Steel
- Crown of All Things New
- Crown of Kingdom Advancement
- Crown of Kingdom Expansion
- Crown of the Lion of the Tribe of Judah

Business Related Crowns

In a recent Heaven Down™ Business prayer meeting, the following crowns were identified and requested:

These are crowns related to business:

- Crown of Abundance
- Crown of Administration
- Crown of Affluence
- Crown of Authority
- Crown of Blessing
- Crown of Blessings of the Lord
- Crown of Business
- Crown of Business Acumen
- Crown of Clarity
- Crown of Courage
- Crown of Deuteronomy 28:1-14
- Crown of Discernment
- Crown of Elevation
- Crown of Faithfulness
- Crown of Favor
- Crown of Financial Commerce
- Crown of Freedom
- Crown of Fruitfulness
- Crown of Glory
- Crown of Health
- Crown of Identity
- Crown of Increased Territory
- Crown of Influence
- Crown of Influence
- Crown of Inheritance
- Crown of Joy
- Crown of Keys
- Crown of Laughter as Medicine
- Crown of Life
- Crown of Might

- Crown of Multiplication
- Crown of Multiplication
- Crown of Networking
- Crown of Occupying
- Crown of Pearls
- Crown of Prosperity
- Crown of Sanctification
- Crown of Sonship
- Crown of Spheres (Spheres of Influence)
- Crown of Stability
- Crown of Stars
- Crown of Steadiness
- Crown of Success
- Crown of the Anointing for Business
- Crown of the Blessings of Father Abraham
- Crown of Trade
- Crown of Understanding
- Crown of Wealth Transfer
- Crown of Wisdom
- Crown of Witty Inventions

———— ∞ ————

Chapter 14

Crown of Wisdom

We stepped into the Library of Revelation and a volume had already been taken from the bookcase and laid on the table. Stephanie sat down at the table as instructed and read the title.

"This is a *Book of Pearls* and these pearls belong to the crowns."

She was instructed that we needed to look at scripture when Wisdom speaks of pearls in the Word. As I was writing this chapter, I searched for the verses in the Word referring to pearls. The first scripture I will reference is found in Matthew 13:45-46:

Matthew 13:45-46:

> [45] *Again, the Kingdom of Heaven is like a merchant seeking beautiful pearls,* [46] *who, when he had found one **pearl of great price**, went*

and sold all that he had and bought it. (Emphasis mine)

She described what she was seeing, "I see two small pearls on top of this book, and I see a piece of a crown, like one of the pieces that would extend up from the crown. What am I to do with this, and who is my teacher?" Across the table, she then saw Moses.

Moses began, "Not only have many sons lost their crowns, but there have been pearls of wisdom that have been scattered to the ground.

The enemy seeks these pearls to devour them, and to keep them from the sons.

"As each son gains a new crown, there is a pearl of wisdom. Seek, and you shall find."

Stephanie asked, "How do we seek, Moses?"

"In the Word, wisdom is found. Have you cast your pearls before swine?" Moses countered.

Matthew 7:6:

*Do not give what is holy to the dogs; nor **cast your pearls before swine**, lest they trample them under their feet, and turn and tear you in pieces. (Emphasis mine)*

Stephanie replied, "Oh, probably yes. I would say that I and others have. If the enemy has come to devour the pearls, and we've cast our pearl before swine, what must we do to retrieve these pearls of wisdom?"

"Many have been in the desert, brought about by their hand because of the loss of a crown and the wisdom it takes to navigate this life through the Word. There are ways to retrieve the pearls and the crowns." Moses responded.

"Okay, can you give me specifics?"

"Are you not called sons?"

"Yes, we are."

Moses then asked, "When you seek, do you find?" He was referring to the next few verses in Matthew.

Stephanie responded affirmatively.

Matthew 7:7-11:

> *⁷ Ask, and it will be given to you; **seek, and you will find;** knock, and it will be opened to you.*

> *⁸ For everyone who asks receives, and he who seeks finds, and to him who knocks it will be opened.*

> *⁹ Or what man is there among you who, if his son asks for bread, will give him a stone?*

> *¹⁰ Or if he asks for a fish, will he give him a serpent?*

> *¹¹ If you then, being evil, know how to give good gifts to your children, how much more will your Father who is in heaven give good things to those who ask Him! (Emphasis mine)*

Moses queried, "Where do you go to find Wisdom?"

"I'm going to assume, but I want you to tell me. I think that we go to her house, and we knock at her door," Stephanie responded.

Proverbs 1:1-3:

> *¹ **Here are kingdom revelations**, words to live by, **and words of wisdom given to empower you to reign in life**, written as proverbs by Israel's King Solomon, David's son. ² Within these sayings will be found the revelation of wisdom and the impartation of spiritual understanding. Use them as keys to unlock the treasures of true knowledge. ³ Those who cling to these words will receive discipline to demonstrate wisdom in every relationship and to choose what is right and just and fair. (TPT) (Emphasis mine)*

Proverbs 21:20-22:

> *²⁰ **In wisdom's house you'll find delightful treasures and the oil of the Holy Spirit.** But the stupid squander what they've been given. ²¹ The lovers of God who chase after righteousness will find all their dreams come*

true: an abundant life drenched with favor and a fountain that overflows with satisfaction. [22] A warrior filled with wisdom ascends into the high place and releases regional breakthrough, bringing down the strongholds of the mighty. (TPT) (Emphasis mine)

Moses answered, "Has Wisdom not invited you to sit at the table?"

"Yes."

"Has your invitation to sit with her regarding LHS's been made available to you?"

Again, Stephanie replied, "Yes."

Moses remarked, "Wisdom is the key. **Repent where you have lost the pearls and thrown them before swine to be devoured by the enemy**, sit with Wisdom, and **she will restore them unto you**."

---

*Every son has a crown that Wisdom creates.
Every pearl is for another crown.*

"This is an interesting statement. I don't understand," Stephanie expressed.

Moses explained, "I did not use Wisdom at the rock. **I not only lost the crown but the authority to come into the promised land.** I cast my pearls before swine."

Any time we don't follow Heaven's instructions; we can lose a crown. In Moses' case, he had been instructed to speak to the rock, but instead, he took his rod and struck the rock as he had done on a prior occasion (which was the instruction then). The result was that the children of Israel got water, but Moses' method was wrong.

Numbers 20:7-12:

> [7] *Then the LORD spoke to Moses, saying,* [8] *'Take the rod; you and your brother Aaron gather the congregation together.* **Speak to the rock** *before their eyes, and it will yield its water; thus you shall bring water for them out of the rock, and give drink to the congregation and their animals.'*
>
> [9] *So Moses took the rod from before the LORD as He commanded him.*
>
> [10] *And Moses and Aaron gathered the assembly together before the rock; and he said to them, 'Hear now, you rebels! Must we bring water for you out of this rock?'*
>
> [11] *Then Moses lifted his hand and struck the rock twice with his rod; and water came out abundantly, and the congregation and their animals drank.*
>
> [12] *Then the LORD spoke to Moses and Aaron,* **'Because you did not believe Me, to hallow**

Me in the eyes of the children of Israel, therefore you shall not bring this assembly into the land which I have given them.' (Emphasis mine)

Moses added, "I did not use Wisdom that day."

"How do you kill the swine to retrieve the pearl?"

"Kill pride. Kill its very essence within you," he answered.

"Moses, we have been working on the generational cleansing of the bloodline, including pride."

Stephanie began praying:

I ask to step into the Courts of Heaven on behalf of myself and my generations, any of us who were prideful and cast our pearls before swine and had pride in our hearts.

We want to repent, and we are requesting a full eradication, a killing of that spirit within us, or the availability for that spirit to work within us as we die to ourselves more and more.

We request that these pearls be gathered and brought back to us and placed upon our crowns as we continue to receive them.

Again, describing what she was seeing, Stephanie said, "I see Wisdom fashioning a crown—a specific crown for each person. She is a part of this process. Thank you, Moses. I feel like this is ending."

"Time is at hand," Moses answered.

Stephanie asked, "May I have my pearl put back and placed into my crown? I see two pearls, and I would like for this to be put on record."

Moses then picked up the piece of the crown she originally saw and realized it was the whole crown. She couldn't see the rest of the crown when it was on the book; she could only see that specific piece where the two pearls should go.

She described, "Moses put them in the crown, and he picked up the full crown—a **Crown of Wisdom**. That is what this is. I see that he's wearing one too.

"Thank you, Moses. He's put my crown on me. I now see this book closing before me and being put back in its space."

---------- ∞ ----------

Chapter 15
The Royal Priesthood of the Crown

In an earlier chapter, we mentioned the Royal Priesthood of the Crown. A demonstration of that was found in the story of Joshua, the High Priest, who had been placed on trial due to accusations of being disqualified from being the High Priest of Jerusalem.

In Zechariah 3:7-8, we read:

> *[7] Thus says the LORD of hosts:*
>
> *1) 'If you will walk in My ways, and*
>
> *2) if you will keep My command, then*
>
> *3) you shall also judge My house, and*
>
> *4) likewise have charge of My courts;*
>
> *5) I will give you places to walk among these who stand here.' (Emphasis mine)*

This passage demonstrates the stewardship expected of Joshua, the High Priest. Satan had charged him with being unqualified to serve as High Priest based on the condition of his garments. A High Priest was required to wear spotless garments, representing a spotless lamb. However, the LORD quickly remedied that for Joshua by ordering him to be clothed with new garments. They even prepared his head for a new crown by placing a turban on his head. The crown would come later, in chapter 6.

In verse 8, we read,

> [8] 'Hear, O Joshua, the high priest, you and your companions who sit before you, for they are a wondrous sign; for behold, I am bringing forth My Servant the BRANCH.'

In chapter 6, we see the rest of this narrative:

Zechariah 6:9-15:

> [9] *Then the word of the LORD came to me, saying:*

> [10] *'Receive the gift from the captives—from Heldai, Tobijah, and Jedaiah, who have come from Babylon—and go the same day and enter the house of Josiah the son of Zephaniah.* [11] *Take the silver and gold,* **make an elaborate crown, and set it on the head of Joshua** *the son of Jehozadak, the high priest.*

> [12] *Then speak to him, saying, 'Thus says the LORD of hosts, saying: 'Behold, the Man whose*

name is the BRANCH! From his place he shall branch out, And he shall build the temple of the LORD; ¹³ yes, He shall build the temple of the LORD. He shall bear the glory, and shall sit and rule on his throne; so he shall be a priest on his throne, and the counsel of peace shall be between them both.'

¹⁴ Now the elaborate crown shall be for a memorial in the temple of the LORD for Helem, Tobijah, Jedaiah, and Hen the son of Zephaniah.

¹⁵ Even those from afar shall come and build the temple of the LORD. Then you shall know that the LORD of hosts has sent Me to you. And this shall come to pass if you diligently obey the voice of the LORD your God. (Emphasis mine)

Once Joshua had proven himself faithful by:

1. Walking in the Father's ways (Zechariah 3:7-8),
2. Keeping His commands,
3. Judging His house,
4. Overseeing the Courts of Heaven under his jurisdiction, and
5. Walking as a son before the personnel of Heaven, including angels, men and women in white, and living creatures.

Then, the dominion of the Royal Priesthood would be bestowed upon him, which we saw in chapter 6, verses 11-12. We know from Peter's epistles that we have been made to be kings and priests.

1 Peter 2:4-10:

> ⁴ *Coming to Him as to a living stone, rejected indeed by men, but chosen by God and precious, ⁵ you also, as living stones, are being built up a spiritual house,* **a holy priesthood**, *to offer up spiritual sacrifices acceptable to God through Jesus Christ.*
>
> ⁶ *Therefore it is also contained in the scripture, 'Behold, I lay in Zion a chief cornerstone, elect, precious, and he who believes on Him will be no means be put to shame.'*
>
> ⁷ *Therefore, to you who believe, He is precious; but to those who are disobedient, 'The stone which the builders rejected has become the chief cornerstone' ⁸ and 'a stone of stumbling and a rock of offense.' They stumble, being disobedient to the word, to which they also were appointed.* ⁹ *But you are a chosen generation,* **a royal priesthood, a holy nation**, *His own special people, that you may proclaim the praises of Him who called you out of darkness into His marvelous light;* ¹⁰ *who once were not a people but are now the people of God, who had not obtained mercy but now have obtained mercy. (Emphasis mine)*

A function of the priest was to stand in the place of the guilty and request absolution for the sins of the people. When we have been crowned with the Crown of Priesthood, we are positioned to do exactly that. We can stand in the gap and forgive sins.

John 20:23:

> *If you forgive the sins of any, they are forgiven them; if you retain the sins of any, they are retained.*

In the arena of forgiveness, where we extend forgiveness (wearing the Crown of Forgiveness), we have an authority in that arena that Satan does not want us to realize—our ability to forgive sins.

---

*The act of forgiveness
removes the hook that was part
of that sin that was forgiven.*

---

*Every sin involves a hook
of some sort.*

That forgiveness creates one less area of dominion that Satan once possessed.

---

*The more we forgive,
the less dominion he has.*

Not only did the High Priest strive to keep the commands of the LORD, but they were also responsible for helping teach the people those commands. With knowledge came understanding and power over the areas of weakness in men's lives.

---

*More areas of freedom
result in fewer areas
of the dominion of Satan.*

———— ∞ ————

Chapter 16

Crown of Bené Elohim

This particular morning, we engaged with Alicia, who serves as our Heavenly Resources Manager. Alicia was sitting at her desk and handed Stephanie a set of three keys. As Stephanie wondered what they were for, she suddenly saw three file folders in front of her. She asked, "What would you like me to understand about these three files and three keys?"

Alicia retorted, "What comes in threes?"

"What comes in threes? Well, I can tell you, Alicia, I've always been told that bad things come in threes," Stephanie quipped.

Alicia laughed and said, "That is what the enemy would like to project. Have you ever come into agreement with that?"

"Yes, I think I have," Stephanie admitted. "It was just an old wives' tale or a superstition. I would like to come out of agreement that bad things come in threes."

Alicia remarked, "What if I was to tell you I gave you **three new keys** to the Kingdom?"

"I would be so excited!"

Stephanie stood up and went over to what usually looked like our bookcase. However, the whole bookcase now looked like it was a door. It was like opening a door in a large home or palace where no one would know there is a door there. There is a whole other set of large volumes here. She asked Alicia, "Is this a different dimension? What is this? What am I looking at?"

Stephanie described what she saw: "These volumes of files are more like the size of a three-ring binder. The space is more expansive, whereas the ones we've always had to see our employee files are small and thin—the ones that have our team's paperwork in them. I see three places that don't have large volumes in them. Two are on one shelf, and another one is below but to the right. What is this?

"I know to take the first key, and I'm putting it in the place where there is no volume. As I opened it, tons and tons of living water began pouring out of it.

"I'm taking the second key and putting it in the second place where there is no volume, and I see wind. I know it is the wind of the Holy Spirit pouring out.

"For the third space, I'm going to use the last key. For some reason, it's tongues. I see the picture of speaking in tongues. We have living water, the wind of the Holy Spirit, and tongues."

Alicia asked, "Would you say that these are three things you've had from the Kingdom of Heaven?"

"She's talking about us as a ministry," Stephanie elucidated. "Yes, we have. But this is new. Will you tell me differently, Alicia, so I can ensure I understand it properly? I am watching these three things pour out—the water, the wind, and the tongues. I see them pouring out, and it's creating a crown in front of me like you see being printed on a 3-D printer. That's what it looks like happening right in front of me. This makes me excited."

I asked, "How does this work, Alicia, for the sons?"

Alicia explained, "Saying 'yes' to the Kingdom is saying 'yes' to the movement of the living water, the very breath of Heaven through His Holy Spirit, and the prayers and tongues that are given to man.

There is an authority
and a right within the sons
as they carry this crown.

"It is lethal in nature against the kingdom of darkness and will be used as public displays. Many hear tongues with the combination and correlation of living water, tongues, and the Spirit behind it—the moves. Water moves, wind moves, and tongues move; The *three* in one accord, the three that are ablaze.

"There are those who have given up their crowns *because of the cost*, but this is the place where you **receive a crown** *because of the cost*. The endurance and the fight that the King has already won, but through the 'yes' of the sons, this crown is given. Unlock, unlock, unlock.

---

*Have the sons receive the keys
and unlock the living water,
the breath of Heaven,
and the tongues.*

Unlock them!

"A 'yes' is involved. It's for the sons," Alicia finished.

Stephanie remarked, "Okay, I'm sitting back in front of her desk. Alicia, it's hard sometimes when people have to start considering the cost."

"The crown outweighs the cost."

The crown outweighs the cost.

"I believe the three files are the three keys needed for this specific crown; it feels like a crown for this age. I don't understand why I'm feeling it this way, but it is for this dimension, for this time," Stephanie spoke. "I ask those three files where I am saying 'yes' to the Kingdom, where Ron and Adina are saying 'yes' to the Kingdom, as this living water, this wind and breath, and the tongues form a crown unlike no other.

"I want those three files to be put on our record and allow us to understand how to teach this to the sons. Is there a scripture about this, Alicia? I just saw a picture of the *Titanic* movie where the man is standing on the deck reading to all of those who know they will die shortly. The scripture, *'and he shall wipe away all their tears'*—that scripture. There's something we need to unlock in that scripture.

Revelation 21:4:

And <u>God will wipe away every tear from their eyes</u>. There shall be no more death nor sorrow, no crying, no more pain, for **the former things have passed away.** *(Emphasis mine)*

Revelation 7:17:

For the lamb, who is in the midst of the throne, will shepherd them, lead them to **fountains of living waters,** *and <u>God will wipe away every tear from their eyes</u>. (Emphasis mine)*

Or...

For the Lamb on the throne will be their Shepherd. He will lead them to springs of life-

> *giving water. And <u>God will wipe every tear from their eyes</u>. (NLT) (Emphasis mine)*

Stephanie exclaimed, "Wow. Fountains of living water!"

I remarked, "We can say that one fits!"

"What is an albatross?" Alicia inquired.

"The albatross is also called a double eagle. It has a huge wingspan. What does that have to do with this?" Stephanie responded.

Alicia queried, "What does the wind do?"

Stephanie remarked, "She is saying we can mount up on wings like eagles. Double the length of our wingspan. That's what this wind is—the Holy Spirit."

Alicia then pointed Stephanie to Acts 2, where the 120 were in the upper room, and cloven tongues like fire sat up each of them.

Alicia asked, "What was on top of their heads?"

Stephanie answered, "Flames of fire!"

"Would that not be a crown?"

"It sounds like it. Alicia!"

I added, "And it lit upon each of them."

Stephanie interjected, "As a crown! I can see it!

Thank you, Father. Lord, we thank you for this crown—for the unlocking of it, the belief system, and the understanding that the living water you are pouring out, the wind of the Holy Spirit, and the tongues are setting in motion a crown that is handcrafted for each of the sons, as they individually say yes.

"No matter where the enemy tries to tell us a lie embedded in fear, there's a cost that causes us to believe it is something we can't bear. It's not true. As we were told in a recent engagement, the term 'consider the cost' is not necessarily what we think.

"Father, we take this beautiful crown. What do we call it? What is the scripture that you read in Revelation?"

I replied, "Revelation 7:17:

> *For the lamb who is in the midst of the throne, will shepherd them and lead them to living fountains of water. And God will wipe away every tear from their eyes.*

"The tears probably have to do with the cost that they thought it carries," I finished.

Stephanie asked, "What is the name of this crown? I hear Holy Spirit say, 'He wore a Crown of Thorns for you.' Is this a crown of cost, Holy Spirit?"

"What is water, wind, and fire?" Alicia questioned.

"Is this a crown of elements?" Stephanie asked. "Not in the elements that He created, but what are water, wind, and fire? Tell me, Holy Spirit. A crown of deity?"

Alicia inquired, "Would you say Father, Son, and Holy Spirit is a deity, three in one?"

"Yes," Stephanie responded.

"Are you three in one?"

"Yes."

Alicia prodded, "Is this crown multifaceted?"

Again, Stephanie replied affirmatively.

Alicia responded, "It has living water, the breath of the Holy Spirit, and tongues."

"Alicia took the three folders and placed two of them inside the other. Okay, I see you. I see you. Do you have to have all three of these or agree with all three of these to have this crown?" Stephanie asked. "How do we differentiate between the many people out there who say that they are God or that they are like God?"

"They are like God—you have been formed in His image, **but** <u>you are not God.</u> You are sons performing his Godhead on Earth as it is in Heaven. Can you take on his deity as sons while you govern?"

"Is that what we do?" Stephanie inquired.

I explained, "Well, we do that when we put on His righteousness. The Father is not seeing earthbound

Stephanie. He's seeing Stephanie the son. He doesn't see all the stuff you've done. He sees a son.

"We're supposed to understand that better as sons. I mean, we are taking on his character.

"We take on His nature. We are *bené elohim*, the sons of God. Bené means son. Elohim is one of the names of God. It is also the name used for the *Just Judge*." I finished.

Alisha asked, "Doesn't that sound like a crown?"

"A bené is a son." I noted. "We are, in essence, considered princes. Think of it in the context of the United Kingdom. We have King Charles and his son Prince William, and then William has children who are princes or princesses. They're the essence of what their father and grandfather carry."

Stephanie exclaimed, "Bené elohim! That's what this crown is, isn't it, because we represent His nature, His deity, and who He is. That's why you were using the word deity, right, Heaven? What a beautiful name for a crown. The LORD God is Elohim (capitalized), we are 'elohim' (not capitalized) and since we are sons of God, we are bené elohim.

"It really struck me when you read that the tears could be because of some of the cost, but they're also saying that the cost isn't necessarily what we thought."

---

*We've been lied to
about some of the costs.*

I added, "Yes, because when He says He will wipe away our tears, that means to obliterate, figuratively, to pardon, blot out, or wipe away."

"Thank you, Lord Jesus. Thank you for wiping away and obliterating our tears with this crown," Stephanie exclaimed. "You obliterate all our tears.

"If we didn't understand it that way, then people would be concerned about the cost. I saw a picture of how we can walk around with a big crown on our head, but we are miserable. Whatever people think will be a cost, you can't walk as a son and be worried about the cost.

---

*You can't walk as a son
and be worried about the cost.*

"That's not how we walk. We walk in authority and confidence that our tears are indeed obliterated and that we've been lied to about the cost by the enemy. Yes, there is a cost. There is some pain and suffering, but it's not what we've thought."

---

*When you are wearing a crown,
you walk differently.*

Stephanie concluded, "You must stand upright to keep it on your head.

We request, in the name of Jesus, that all of our contractors, our employees, our intercessors, and all those that are part of you (Ron) in this office, Alicia (you being over them), would receive the three keys and that they be put on their record for them to then take, as an act of faith, open up these three areas in this different dimension and receive this Crown of the Bené Elohim.

———— ∞ ————

Chapter 17

The Superior Crown

The morning following the Crown of the Bené Elohim revelation, I heard the following as I spent time before the Lord:

> *More understanding is coming for the Crowns book. As you keep digging, revelation will unfold. I have much to share with My sons on the subject. I want them to understand the crowns and the dominion they possess as sons. It is not just a cute concept but life-changing for those who embrace what I'm doing in this day and hour.*

---

*Crowns are critical
for the sons to understand.*

> *Much more is alluded to about crowns than you even imagine yet. Authority in one's life can be reborn or reignited by the embrace of crowns.*

> Some crowns come **with** a cost,
> and others come
> **because** of the cost.

Just as you learned about bonds, the number of crowns available to My sons is immeasurable, for I want their authority to be immeasurable.

Yesterday, you saw the tongues of fire alighting upon the heads of the 120 in the upper room, with crowns placed upon their heads; other demonstrations of crowns being placed upon someone are scattered throughout scripture. When the Crown of Fire sat upon the heads of the 120, it ignited a revelation that would impact the entire globe. It was not a Crown of Drunkenness as they were accused of, but rather one of landscape-changing expression of the power of God.

When healing was demonstrated in the book of Acts with the man at the temple gate who had been lame, Peter and John carried a Crown of Wholeness, and as they said, 'Such as I have, I give to you,' the wholeness they possessed was passed to the cripple, and the infirmity in his body bowed to the authority of the Crown of Wholeness. In every instance where healing or miracles manifested, it demonstrated an inferior crown bowing to a Superior Crown. The sick man was wearing a Crown of Sickness, and it needed to be exchanged for a Crown of Wholeness.

*When people carry a Crown of Depression or Defeat, those inferior crowns **must** bow to the Superior Crown of Hope and Victory. When you see how many are bent low under the weight of an inferior crown, now see that inferior crown bowing to a Superior Crown. That is how healing manifests and how labels are defeated in people's lives.*

Many come to LifeSpring weighed down by the label of an inferior crown. All they need to do is replace that inferior crown with a Superior Crown. Remember, My Word says that, in the name of Jesus, every knee will bow, and every tongue will confess the Lordship of Jesus. That is an inferior crown bowing to the Superior Crown.

The Authority of Inferior Crowns

A principle of the Word is that all crowns carry a degree of authority related to the type of crown they are. Therefore, if someone has received a Crown of Sickness, that crown will begin to manifest sickness of some sort in the person's body. As you, as sons, learn to facilitate the exchange of inferior crowns with Superior Crowns, healing will manifest because a Crown of Wholeness carries with it the authority to release wholeness into a person, thereby defeating the operation of the Crown of Sickness. We have already discussed how crowns are representative of the authority one carries in a particular arena.

Crowns are representative of the authority we carry in a particular arena.

When you, as a son, read authority-related verses, understand that the inferior is bowing to the superior.

You have only scratched the surface in learning about these matters. As the sons embrace the power and authority of this revelation, they will be filled with the ability to shape every landscape impacted by inferior crowns.

As the sons exercise the authority in the various crowns they carry, many who have been weighed down under the weight of inferior crowns will find those crowns coming off their heads and being replaced by the Superior Crown.

Every capability of the Father can be released and made resident in a crown. For healing, you have the expression of Jehovah Raphe (The Lord our Healer), for provision (Jehovah Jireh), for victory in battle, Jehovah Sabaoth (the Lord of Hosts), and more. His touch is in everything He has created. The crowns lack nothing.

The Superior Crown of 1 Corinthians 13

In 1 Corinthians 13, you see the inferior bowing to the Superior Crown of Love.

1 Corinthians 13:1-13:

> *[1] If I could speak all the languages of earth and of angels, but didn't love (a Superior Crown) others, I would only be a noisy gong or a clanging cymbal (the sound of inferior crowns).*
>
> *[2] If I had the gift of prophecy, and if I understood all of God's secret plans and possessed all knowledge, and if I had such faith that I could move mountains, but didn't love (operate under the Superior Crown) others, I would be nothing.*
>
> *[3] If I gave everything I have to the poor (poverty is an inferior crown) and even sacrificed my body, I could boast (an inferior crown) about it; but if I didn't love (operate from the Superior Crown) others, I would have gained nothing.*

⁴ Love (the Superior Crown) is patient and kind. Love is not jealous or boastful or proud ⁵ or rude. (expressions of inferior crowns) It does not demand its own way (an inferior crown). It is not irritable (another inferior crown), and it keeps no record of being wronged (yet another inferior crown).

⁶ It does not rejoice about injustice (an inferior crown) but rejoices whenever the truth wins out (the result of wearing a Superior Crown).

⁷ Love never gives up, never loses faith, is always hopeful, and endures through every circumstance (as you operate from the authority of a Superior Crown).

⁸ Prophecy and speaking in unknown languages and special knowledge will become useless. But love (the Superior Crown) will last forever!

⁹ Now our knowledge is partial and incomplete (as it is from an inferior crown), and even the gift of prophecy reveals only part of the whole picture!

¹⁰ But when the time of perfection comes (when the sons all walk in the authority of the Superior Crown), these partial things will become useless.

¹¹ When I was a child, I spoke and thought and reasoned as a child. But when I grew up, I put away childish things.

¹² Now, we see things imperfectly, like puzzling reflections in a mirror, but then we will see everything with perfect clarity (because we are viewing them from the authority of a Superior Crown). All that I know now is partial and incomplete, but then I will know everything completely, just as God now knows me completely.

¹³ Three things will last forever—faith, hope, and love—and the greatest of these is love (the Superior Crown). (NLT) (Emphasis mine)

As the sons choose to walk in the authority of the Superior Crown of love—the Superior Crown, landscapes will change, lives will change, and expressions and responses will change. You will respond differently to situations when you put on the Superior Crown. You will respond differently to people. You will react differently!

Imagine a body of believers who choose to walk in the authority of the Superior Crown of Love. How different would their landscape be? How different would their neighborhood be? When they see sickness or disease, they facilitate a *change from an inferior crown to the Superior Crown.*

Remember Matthew 10:1:

> *Jesus called his twelve disciples together and gave them **authority** to cast out evil spirits and to heal every kind of disease and illness. (NLT) (Emphasis mine)*

In the natural arena, Jesus simply laid hands on them and gave them authority, but in the spirit, He placed a crown upon them that caused evil spirits (LHS's under assignment), diseases, and illnesses to bow as inferior crowns to the Superior Crowns they carried.

A few verses later, Jesus expands on the authority He gave them.

Matthew 10:5-14:

> *⁵ Jesus sent out the twelve apostles with these instructions: 'Don't go to the Gentiles or the Samaritans (it isn't time to go to them yet), ⁶ but only to the people of Israel—God's lost sheep.*
>
> *⁷ 'Go and announce to them that the Kingdom of Heaven is near (the Superior Crown has arrived!).*
>
> *⁸ 'Heal the sick, raise the dead, cure those with leprosy, and cast out demons. Give as*

freely as you have received! (The authority came because Jesus came. The inferior crowns of sickness, death, leprosy, and demonic oppression must now bow to those carrying Superior Crowns.)

⁹ 'Don't take any money in your money belts—no gold, silver, or even copper coins. ¹⁰ Don't carry a traveler's bag with a change of clothes and sandals or even a walking stick. Don't hesitate to accept hospitality because those who work deserve to be fed. (Watch the inferior Crown of Need bow to the Superior Crown of provision.)

¹¹ 'Whenever you enter a city or village, search for a worthy person and stay in his home until you leave town. ¹² When you enter the home, give it your blessing (releasing the blessing that is resident in the Superior Crown you carry.) ¹³ If it turns out to be a worthy home, let your blessing stand; if it is not, take back the blessing. ***(The blessing of a Superior Crown can be released, and it can be called back.)***

¹⁴ 'If any household or town refuses to welcome you or listen to your message, shake its dust from your feet as you leave. (For those places hostile to the Superior

Crown, don't leave any of the residue of blessing on that household or town.)' (NLT) (Emphasis mine)

> You are responsible for the stewardship of the blessing contained in a particular crown.

As you learn to walk and work from the authority of a Superior Crown, much will change. When you look in a mirror, see yourself carrying Superior Crowns.

In Luke 10:19, Jesus is speaking and says:

Look, I have given you authority (of a Superior Crown) over all the power (inferior crowns) of the enemy, and you can walk among snakes and scorpions (operations of inferior crowns) and crush them. Nothing will injure you. (NLT) (Emphasis mine)

Have you noticed that when we lay hands on someone to pray for them, we generally lay hands upon their head? We are essentially crowning them with whatever it is you are praying for them about or imparting to them.

These changes can apply to every arena of your life. Step into the Court of Crowns and receive what I have to say and receive the authority of *the Superior Crowns for the sons you are, and as sons, you will demonstrate a superior Kingdom. The time is now!*

───── ∞ ─────

Chapter 18

Crown of the Bride

As Stephanie and I accessed the Library of Revelation, we were met by the Apostle Peter. Peter was seated at a table and we could hear the words, "To Him who sits on the throne and unto the lamb be blessing and honor and glory and power forever." As Stephanie approached the other side of the table, Peter stood, kissed her cheeks, and greeted her.

Stephanie replied in kind and asked, "What do you want to teach us today?"

Peter began, "You have heard of the simplicity of the gospel, but there are facets of the gospel that are complex in nature. It is indeed a mystery, and this is where the mystery unfolds.

Let the readers know
they are invited into
the Library of Revelation.

"Each one of them *has their own library*, but they must steward this as the Lord wants to pour out the understanding of the mysteries. There is a mystery in Revelation."

"I understand that the word 'revelation' is dual here—the Spirit of Revelation and the Book of Revelation," Stephanie responded.

Peter added, "And the complexity is only for those *who do not* steward well."

Stephanie paused and asked, "Can I stop you right there, Peter? When you say that, what does that mean? Are you talking about relationship?"

"Yes, relationship. The Library of Revelation is for those who seek a deeper relationship with Him. With intimacy comes relationship. With relationship comes the key to the door of the Library of Revelation."

"What is complex resolution? I just heard that." She countered.

Peter explained, "It's where inferiority is removed, and exceptionalism meets understanding. You are exceptional in your sonship and in who you are."

Embrace the complexity of sonship, and it will be opened to you.

"You know me, Peter," Stephanie spoke. "I feel like we're talking in riddles a little bit. Help us understand."

Peter elucidated, "How many of you have been taught that the only ones who could read and understand the Word are those who are Christians? How many times have you read a scripture you have read before, and at that specific time, something new awakens in you? It's the same concept."

He began showing her all of the volumes of books in the bookcases and she noted, "This place is special, isn't it, Peter?"

Peter agreed, "He (Jesus) is in every volume. This is where kings search a matter out."[13]

"What would you have us search out today, Peter?"

"Complexities."

"Of course."

Peter went to the bookcase, selected a huge volume, and opened it up. It was a pop-up book like children often have. As he opened it, a crown popped up.

Stephanie remarked how hilariously Heaven talks to her sometimes, like using a children's pop-up book.

Peter replied, "I knew you would like that."

---

[13] Proverbs 25:2 It is the glory of God to conceal a matter, but the glory of kings is to search out a matter.

"Well, we must come as little children to understand, so teach me."

As she began turning the pages, she realized a different and new crown popped up with each page. They would "rise to the top." As she turned each page, there was another crown and another crown."

He explained, "This library is where Ron gets his information for the book. It has already been written in Heaven."

"I wish that we, in the natural, could see as we speak about a crown how it literally pops up (rises to the top), and each one is so different and unique. Each of them has a different scale," Stephanie described. "I just turned the page again, and there is one with jewels. Every jewel is a ruby. Everything is red. Am I to know what this crown is because it sticks out to me? It's beautiful."

"This is a Crown for the Bride," Peter clarified.

Stephanie exclaimed, "Wow! Will each crown be unique to the person—the bride—the Crown for the Bride? That's my first question. My second question is: will we receive this in the future?"

He expounded, "Each crown is unique to the individual. This is *your* crown, Stephanie."

Each crown is unique to the individual.

Stephanie said, "I feel the sense that he is urging the people to come, sit, and take this Book of Crowns, open it until they come to the Crown for the Bride. It is unique to them, and I realize we can receive it now."

As she spoke, the Book of Crowns turned from what had been a pop-up into an actual crown. As she picked it up, she could feel its weight. She needed to ask about the rubies because they were made of rubies. As she placed it on her head, she said, "Tell me more, Peter."

Peter replied, "You *are* the Bride of Christ. Now, *be* the bride. Honor your husband (Jesus). Honor the crown. There will be tangible evidence of the authority."

She noted that Heaven has been spoken to us about "BE" for at least two years.

She asked, "Peter, you walk under this crown here in Heaven, but as a man, is it difficult for men to understand being a bride? For women, it's easy. I think men can understand the complexity of the authority, but can they understand being a bride? To understand sitting *under* His authority, well, that's another matter."

Having this crown
gives you a seat of authority
that not all carry.
Men can understand authority.

Stephanie explained that she felt she was supposed to look up the word 'bride.' I think there are multiple meanings associated with the bride, but they are always related to a woman, except in the Bible.

According to the bibledictionarytoday.com:

> *The term bride carries profound, significant symbolism in the union of two individuals and in reflecting more profound spiritual truths about the relationship between God and His people. It transcends mere marital definitions. It serves as a metaphor for faith, commitment, and divine love. It symbolizes a faithful partner, one who enters into a sacred relationship.*
>
> *Revelation 19:7-8 states, 'Let us rejoice in Him, be glad and give Him glory for the wedding of the lamb has come and His bride has made herself ready. Fine linen, bright and clean, was given her to wear. It underscores the anticipation of the ultimate union between Christ and the church, which symbolizes hope and redemption.'*[14]

Stephanie asked, "Peter, what else do you want us to know about this?"

---

[14] Bibledictionarytoday.com/words/bride

"It is in a deep, intimate relationship that this crown is received."

"I am stuck in this moment of looking at this crown and realizing its weightiness. Not that it's a hard crown to wear; it's not heavy, but the understanding that not everyone gets this crown—that is what is heavy. This comes with authentic intimacy with Jesus. I mean, we are supposed to be the bride of Christ.

"Heaven is giving me the imagery of the 10 women with the lamps who were supposed to be preparing. Not everyone received the King. He wants *all* to receive this crown.

This crown does come with a cost— the cost of intimacy.

"That's why there's a weightiness to this crown. I see you now, Peter, with this crown. There's a reverence here regarding this crown."

She heard Peter say, "Many are called, but few are chosen."[15]

She remarked, "I never liked that scripture."

I added, "Very simply, not everybody will do what it takes. He has offered it out to a lot of people."

---

[15] Matthew 22:14

Stephanie inserted, "He has given me the understanding that He has offered it to a lot of people, but the revelation in the book that you're writing will help solidify it for an innumerable number of people. This ministry will help many people become brides and receive this crown. I am overcome with His love for the people."

I closed, saying, "Thank you, Peter."

"Thank you, Peter. I have to look up rubies and find out their significance," she added.

After a quick search, we found that rubies symbolize love, passion, protection, and wealth. They are traditional wedding gifts and symbolize everlasting affection.

Stephanie was stunned. "You can't make that up. Thank you, Father. Of course, it symbolizes weddings. He knew I would need that. Wow! What's funny is that I've never really been a big fan of rubies. Now I am!"

———— ∞ ————

Chapter 19

Crowns of Conquest

I had wondered about how crowns affect geographical regions, so Heaven provided some insights concerning that, primarily from the book of Joshua.

> *As a son, you are a prince, and princes have crowns that are for designated regions of the Earth. Where I have pre-appointed the times and boundaries of your dwelling places, just as Joshua understood the boundaries of areas they had conquered, Joshua had the Crown of Leadership over the children of Israel. Look at Joshua and see the different crowns he carried throughout his lifetime. I told him that EVERY place that the soul of his foot would tread, I had given to them. In Joshua 1:4, I defined the territory he was to eventually conquer. As he conquered, he was to distribute to the various tribes as their inheritance. The sons have not*

well understood inheritance, but crowns are a part of that package. Joshua was given instructions concerning not letting the Law of God be forgotten in his life.

Some of the children of Israel had been promised inheritance on one side of the Jordan River but were instructed to send their men to assist their brothers in the conquest of the unoccupied lands.

Sometimes, you will be required to assist another in gaining their inheritance before enjoying your own.

Sometimes, your assignment is to assist another in their conquest.

In Joshua 2, the king of Jericho was informed that Joshua had sent spies into his territory. The Jerichoites had heard of their conquests under Moses against the Amorites and fear had gripped them. Moses had possessed a Crown of Conquest that now rested upon Joshua.

> *When conquest is in your future,*
> *the Lord will cause your enemies*
> *to fear you.*

As recorded in Joshua 3:4, the army of Israel was going to have to do things never done before and go through unfamiliar places. You will experience the same thing as you go forth to conquer.

> *Also, a time of preparation*
> *will be required*
> *before conquest is realized.*

The Lord used the event of drying up the Jordan River so the armies could cross over to establish that Joshua, their leader, was indeed anointed by God for the task.

> *The Lord will always have someone*
> *appointed to lead the conquest.*

In Joshua 5, we find that the preparation times may be painful but necessary.

> *Times of preparation*
> *are not times for battle.*

As the children of Israel finished their preparations, what they had relied on for sustenance in the past was no longer sufficient. They had to rely on the sustenance provided in the new locale.

Your diet may change with a new location.

In Joshua 5:13, the angel assigned to assist Joshua makes himself known. He is not an angel of provision but a conquering angel.

Angels will always be assigned to the conquering assignment you possess.

The angel brought the strategy for the conquest of Jericho.

Always <u>only move</u> with strategy.

In Joshua 6, we see that the process of conquest is not always pretty. It cost the enemies all they had.

> Never partake of accursed things
> in a place of conquest.

In chapter 7, the disobedience of one affected the entire camp of the children of Israel.

> Private sin can have
> public consequences.

The method of conquest may be different from previous methods. Always follow the instructions of those in charge.

In Joshua 8, Joshua built an altar to the Lord to honor the conquest of Ai where Joshua worshipped before the Lord.

Imposters may come before you. Always seek the counsel of the Lord and not be moved by your emotions (see Joshua 9:14). The Gibeonites came to Joshua under false pretenses. The result was...

> Those who deceive you
> may become your servants.

In Joshua 10, we find the resources of Heaven (hailstones) are used to assist in the battle. Joshua commanded the elements to cooperate with the army of Israel, and they obeyed (see

Joshua 10:12-13). Just like Joshua, you want the Lord to fight your battles (v. 14).

In Joshua 10:25, Joshua expresses a promise that is ours today:

> Then Joshua said to them, 'Do not be afraid, nor be dismayed; be strong and of good courage, for thus the LORD will do to all your enemies against whom you fight.'

Each of the kings who chose to fight against Joshua lost their crowns, their dominion, and their place of authority.

Each crown designates a place of dominion. Joshua was operating under a dominion that included the entire land of Canaan. What is your place of dominion?

In chapter 11, we find the principle that no matter the alliances of those coming against you, when the LORD fights your battles, He will win.

Another principle of conquest is found in Joshua 11:15:

> As the LORD had commanded Moses, his servant, so Moses commanded Joshua, and **so Joshua did. He left nothing undone of all that the LORD had commanded Moses.** *(Emphasis mine)*

One of the reasons for the absolute destruction of the many people the army of Israel killed was because they were polytheistic and believed and worshipped many gods, while Israel only worshipped the LORD God Jehovah. The LORD did not want the Israelites contaminated by pagan worship.

In Joshua 11:23, we read:

> *So Joshua took the whole land, according to all that the LORD had said to Moses, and Joshua gave it as an inheritance to Israel according to their divisions by their tribes.* ***Then, the land rested from war.*** *(Emphasis mine)*

Conquests will always cost you something. The Superior Crown of those commissioned by the LORD will always be victorious over the inferior crowns of your enemies. The many kings that came against Israel represented different things that had to be destroyed in the lives of the people.

That is why the times of preparation are essential. You cannot leave anything undone and never exit the time of preparation prematurely. Just as the LORD was with Joshua, so He will be with you. Wear the Crown of the Conqueror and take the land allotted to you for the Kingdom.

The LORD granted an extended period of rest to Joshua and the Israelites. However, he was not quite done conquering within his territory. He still had lands to take possession of.

Don't confuse a respite
with a release from an instruction.

Caleb, who had helped spy out the land earlier, still had the Crown of a Conqueror in his possession, and he would not let age or vigor stand in his way.

The balance of the book of Joshua has to do with the division of the land among the twelve tribes of Israel. Each tribe had a specific portion of the overall territory allotted to the Israelites. Each portion had blessings and anointings that could be capitalized for the benefit of the inhabitants. Wherever the LORD has placed you, you have specific blessings and anointings you are to capitalize on as sons. Wear the crown and possess the land, for it is the gift of the LORD to you.

It is interesting that in Joshua 12:9-24, we find that Joshua conquered 31 kings in total.

Take the lessons from this chapter and apply them to your jurisdiction.

Proverbs 21:22

***A warrior filled with wisdom ascends into the high place and releases regional breakthrough,** bringing down the strongholds of the mighty. (TPT) (Emphasis mine)*

———— ∞ ————

Chapter 20
Crown of Creativity

Stephanie began our engagement, saying,

Father, thank you for the opportunity to step into the realms of Heaven. We glorify your name, and we praise you, Jesus. Thank you. Thank you for the restoration of all things. Crowns, sonship, realms of Heaven, we praise Your name.

We ask to step into the realms of Heaven as little children. We invite the Seven Spirits of God, Wisdom, Knowledge, Understanding, the Spirit of Revelation, Counsel, Might, the Spirit of the Lord, and the Reverential Fear of the Lord. We invite every man and woman in white. I commission my angels to co-labor and be a part of this.

She then asked, "What do it we need to do today? What does Heaven have to say today?"

She began describing what she was perceiving, which was the Help Desk. This time, however, it had a hole in the front of the desk that a child could crawl through. Since, in this engagement, she was a little girl, she stepped through the hole and into a Creativity Room. She could see all kinds of different stations where people were working. There were seamstresses, people fashioning with wood and iron, and other stations of creativity, too.

"Why has Heaven brought me here today?" She inquired.

Malcolm was our teacher for the moment and he responded, "There's an Uncommon Room of Productivity, but there's also an Uncommon Room of Creativity."

"How interesting and delightful," she remarked. "Thank you, Lord. The more I look at this, the more I realize that instead of stepping *into* this room, I view it in an unusual way. It is as if I was looking through a glass bubble. You can step towards something and into that bubble to view things. It looks like that because the image is distorted. It is as if I am looking through a lens. What can we do in this Uncommon Room of Creativity? What question am I supposed to ask?"

Malcolm asked, "Has creativity been lost?"

"I would say, 'No,' but I know Heaven has an answer."

"Can something be lost that has not truly been found?"

Stephanie answered, "So it's not lost. We just haven't discovered something or come to the fullness of it. Malcolm, how is something lost that hasn't yet been found? Regarding creativity, we don't know the full spectrum of it yet. Is that what you're saying?"

"The Creator has instilled in every son the ability to create. It is through this lens of imagination that He speaks," he responded.

The Creator has instilled in every son the ability to create. It is through this lens of imagination that He speaks.

Stephanie noted, "That's why I'm seeing this through a lens right now. I get it. There have been a lot of people who are super creative. Malcolm reminds me that Heaven just said the Father has put creativity in every person. I know many people who say they don't have a creative bone; I do know that there are people who believe that. What does this have to do with LifeSpring?"

Malcolm replied,

> *There are creative resources*
> *within every son;*
> *they only need to ask.*

"It will be different for each person. There is a Crown of Creativity.

"Why is this important? Within the Crown of Creativity, there are markers in time. Have you ever heard of the saying, 'This is a lost art?' That is a marker in time.

"Have the sons take the Crown of Creativity, for there are many things that the Lord wants to release upon the Earth through the sons and not through mere man.

> *The things that have been stolen*
> *from the sons in creativity*
> *are now being returned*
> *through the Crown of creativity*
> *given by the Great Creator Himself.*

"The *majesty* with which He chooses to bring creativity through the sons will level. This will level the playing field.

> *Sons are created to be
> masters of many things
> because that's what sonship bears.*

"There is a unique design for every son in each crown. *Pick up your crowns.*"

> *Pick up your crowns.*

Stephanie remarked, "Okay. What an interesting concept. As I turned away from this lens that I was looking through, I saw a crown on the Help Desk. I don't know enough about gemstones, but everything about it is sapphire blue.

"I will pick up my Crown of Creativity and put it on. Heaven is giving me this understanding; so many creative things the Father wanted to give through his sons would bring wealth. Creative things had to come to the Earth, and many times, they did not come through the sons. They came through mere man, and the sons lost out—*we* lost out on some things."

I commented to Stephanie, "Sapphires are associated with wisdom, spiritual enlightenment, and enhanced communication skills."

She observed, "I guess creativity can come in communication skills, too."

"It was also part of the breastplate for the priest, for the high priest. It was the second stone in the second row," I noted.

"What a gift to be given a crown <u>from The Creator</u>. The one who creates."

"And the ones that say they don't have a creative bone in their body, is that because a crown was stolen?" I asked.

"It has to be," she responded. "It would make sense that He would give every single son a type or form of creativity. It doesn't have to mean drawing, painting, or singing. It can be many things. All the trades were devalued because you can be super creative by finding any problem with the mechanics of a car to fix it. That's creativity.

"The creativity for each of us has something so dynamic that as we bring it, it brings us wealth. A lot of creativity has gone to wicked people because He needed to bring an idea, an invention, to the Earth for us to be able to have something, and if the sons didn't want it, he gave it to somebody who would take it."

She noted about Malcolm, "He has his crown on. Thank you, Malcolm. I'm excited.

"Think about the words we say. Crowns and words really do correlate because for people to say, 'I don't have a creative bone in my body,' is an actual agreement. They are in agreement with a false verdict that needs to be overturned."

———— ∞ ————

Chapter 21

Crowns in a Storm

As we engaged Heaven to meet with our Chief Angel, Ezekiel, Stephanie heard the phrase, "Calm before the storm," but then Ezekiel went further, saying, "But *in* storms, there is a calm."

Stephanie then had a vision of someone casting a crown into a storm, and the storm immediately became calm. In addition to casting our crowns at Jesus' feet, we can also figuratively cast our crowns (and the authority they represent) into a storm, causing the storm to settle.

It's another means of governing for the sons.

We, as sons, can step into a storm and, with the Superior Crown of Jesus, bring peace into the storm.

*It is not a loss of a crown,
it's an expression of the dominion
of a crown.*

*Simply commission angels to step in
to pull down the frequencies
of storms as you release
your crown into the storm.*

It is part of our co-laboring with the angels.

*To those who have and wear the Superior Crowns, you can not only be the calm **before** the storm, but you can also be the calm **in** the storm.*

*You can step into others' storms.
and speak to cause the calming
of the raging seas.*

This is a governing tool and technique but can only be done under the Superior Crown. Expect storms to subside as you walk in this new manifold expression of his love. This is a part of the quieting, which is a tool/weapon angels use to settle situations down.

> *As sons, we can step ahead*
> *in time and calm storms*
> *before their scheduled arrival,*
> *so we don't have to contend*
> *with the aggravation of the storm.*

When we step ahead in time, see a storm, then release a Superior Crown into that storm, causing it to settle before it even gets started. Remember to co-labor with the angels to accomplish this.

The prior afternoon, during a session, we were experiencing a lot of distractions and I governed the distractions with quieting.

> *We can cast a Superior Crown*
> *into ANY storm*
> *and watch the storm dissipate.*

We asked how we could teach this for the sake of the people because we know the Bible has dual meanings.

Stephanie then saw a picture of the disciples in the boat while Jesus was asleep. Even though the Superior Crown was in the boat with them, the storm still came. When the authority of that crown was used and measured, the storm was quelled.

> *As we sit under
> the Superior Crown
> and use our words,
> the storms will cease.*

As we sit under the authority of the Superior Crown, we can have it co-labor with our angels and the angels of this ministry to go ahead of time to any storm and introduce calm before the storm. We can speak to all storms that would come in advance and, by working with the angels, instruct all inferior crowns to bow to the Superior Crown. The frequency of all storms is cast to the ground. All the storms in advance go unnoticed because they have already been quelled.

Angels, we choose to co-labor with you as we move ahead of time and as you have us help sense the calm before the storm, and we use this as an advanced technique of the crowns to co-labor with you and pull down all storms that would come in the name of Jesus.

Father, we thank you for being the light that breaks through all darkness, and we speak that all raging seas must be calm. We speak peace. What you reign in is peace. Thank you, Father. Thank you, Ezekiel.

Speaking to Ezekiel, Stephanie continued:

Ezekiel, we co-labor with you to calm any storm that would come toward LifeSpring and all components of it; that you would help the intercessors understand this;

that we understand it, and that we co-labor together, so that every inferior crown in every storm must bow its knee to the Superior Crown in the name of Jesus.

Stephanie could see Ezekiel having fun. He was personally using crowns and throwing them into storms. The crown was like a boomerang, coming back to him.

When Paul was in the storm,[16] he used the authority of the Superior Crown he possessed to dominate the inferior Crown of the Storm. He governed the storm so no loss of life occurred so long as the occupants of the boat obeyed Paul's instructions. We can do similarly and govern storms before they arrive so that the storms don't arrive.

———— ∞ ————

---

[16] Acts 27:13-38

Chapter 22

Every Crown Has a Mantle

We came to the Help Desk to find out what it was that Heaven had for us that day. Malcolm, our tutor, was standing and leaning on the Help Desk with his feet crossed in a casual stance. Stephanie greeted him, and he promptly placed something on her left shoulder.

"What is this on my shoulder?" she asked.

"It's a chip," he replied.

Stephanie responded, "So—you're going to talk about chips on our shoulders."

Malcolm then knocked it off and put another chip on her shoulder, and an angel knocked it off.

She asked, "What are we doing here? What's this about?"

With a grin, he placed another chip on her shoulder, which grew to a mantle. She had to take the mantle off her shoulders because of the weight of it.

He explained, "There are mantles to be picked up just like crowns. What would you say if the coincidence around a chip being placed on a shoulder at the exact moment a mantle was to fall is indeed no coincidence at all? The enemy is afraid of crowns but he's more afraid of mantles."

With crowns,
you walk in your authority;
with mantles,
you assert your authority.

Stephanie remarked, "Well, I see this one chip on my shoulder. What do I need to do about it?"

She suddenly knew who this chip represented. Stephanie explained that she had been going into Heaven and talking to Heaven about a particular situation. However, she understood she indeed had a chip on her shoulder regarding this person in her life. She continued, "Malcolm, I feel like I've come into Heaven, and I have repented of these things, and I've forgiven this person. Is there a mantle that needs to be picked up?"

"Yes, there is, but the chip is still there. You have to deal with the chip first."

Stephanie prayed a very private prayer regarding this person, even having compassion regarding them in the end.

She then had a question for Malcolm: "My question to you, Malcolm, is, 'As a child, I was receiving a mantle. What was that mantle?'"

"I don't know, pick it up," he directed her.

The Mantle of Receiving Love from Your Parents

Stephanie could see it at her feet, so she reached down, picked it up, and put it on her shoulders.

She remarked, "This is a Mantle of Receiving Love from Your Parents. Wow! I bet many kids had this one knocked off their shoulders, or it couldn't land."

"There is a special mantle for children that they are to carry," Malcolm explained. "The love that is supposed to be given by the parents is in this mantle. With this mantle, you can walk in the assuredness, the surety, and the receiving of the love of a father and of a mother that is healthy and pure. It's a mantle of comfort. Many don't have this mantle, but the Lord restores all."

Stephanie prayed,

Father, I thank you for this mantle, and I ask to step back into time when I was to receive this mantle from you. I know it was given to me at birth, too, and I had that mantle. I see that it was on me as a baby, but here it's as if this mantle had outgrown the other one, and the new one was to be established, and I missed it, or it came off my shoulders because of this chip.

Malcolm explained, "Think about this. This mantle is being hindered from landing because of a chip on your shoulder. Maintaining a mantle of a parent's love and comfort would be difficult if you no longer trust it. Let it be reestablished in you. With it will come the comfort and the love—a reestablishment of that parental love."

Stephanie noted. "I was just thinking about all the children whose parents gave them away.

"Yes, they are missing this mantle."

"Can you tell me why this mantle is important now that we're adults?"

He began, "Without this mantle, receiving love from anyone is very difficult. Many hold others at arm's length. Many have difficulty being a parent and refuse the Father's love. So—have it reestablished, and reestablishment shall come."

"Is this like how when we walk into the Court of Crowns, there is a reestablishment of the authority of crowns? Is there a particular court?"

"With a crown comes a mantle. When you receive a crown, you are not only receiving a crown, but also its mantle."

> *With a crown comes a mantle.*
> *When you receive a crown,*
> *not only are you receiving a crown,*
> *you are receiving its mantle.*

Stephanie prayed:

I ask to step into the Court of Crowns to receive my Crown of Parental Love and Comfort, my mantle, and the authority that comes with it to be reestablished into my life.

"Malcolm, how does this work for those who were adopted or whose parents may have let them live with them, but they abuse them?" she asked.

"It is the same," he replied. "This is for their healing. This is for their reestablishment and feeling like a human being—feeling love.

"The enemy came to kill, steal, and destroy, and he has sought to destroy the family unit by taking the crowns and the mantles at a very young age, creating accusations and unforgiveness. It has kept humanity from walking in wholeness with authority and the re-establishment of them as sons and daughters.

"The first point of contact for a human, as designed by the Father, is through the parent. That is why the enemy has roared like a lion. Destroy what he has been doing. Be empowered to re-establish this in people's lives."

She remarked, "I see that we cannot do this without true forgiveness to all who have wounded us deeply. That is why we cannot have a chip on our shoulders when we come here.

Father, I pray that many will be reestablished into wholeness from this mantle being placed back on the shoulders and this Crown of Nurture and Being Nurtured being handed to us.

"Malcolm, I want to be sure of the name of this. I see its value, especially for so many who lost a parent in childbirth, whose parents gave them away, or who lived in abusive, horrific situations where their first understanding of love through a parent was not as it was supposed to be.

"This feels like a wrap-around love," she observed.

Psalms 32:10:

> *But when you trust in the Lord for forgiveness,* **his wrap-around love will surround you.** *(TPT) (Emphasis mine)*

Psalms 61:3

> *Lord, you are a paradise of protection to me. You lift me high above the fray. None of my foes can touch me when* **I'm held firmly in your wrap-around presence!** *(TPT) (Emphasis mine)*

People often say, "I know He loves me, but I can't experience it." *That is a mantle that has been lost.* This crown was gone because we are supposed to give our children the picture of the Father's love in an unconditional, loving manner towards a newborn and children.

Thank you, Father, for this crown and this mantle. I know many mantles will coincide with the crowns we receive. I ask for an establishment of all mantles for the crowns I've received to date to be placed upon my shoulder in this wrap-around love that I feel here in this court—the authority that it gives us and the reestablishment of it.

Stephanie remarked, "I feel like the next piece of this will be the reestablishment of our thrones. Thank you, your Honor. He's showing me that here, I see a layer of my mantle, and I'm placing it around my mom. Because I received it, I give it. Just like Peter and John in the Book of Acts, where they said, 'Silver and gold, I don't have, but what I do have, I give to you.' I give you this because I know you missed out on this, too.

I ask for her to have a Crown of Nurture put back on her head.

Colossians 3:21 says,

> *Fathers do not provoke your children less they become discouraged.*

That is when some chips can come on your shoulder. One translation says, 'Fathers, do not exasperate your children so that they will not lose heart.'

2 Timothy 1:5:

> For I am mindful of the sincere faith within you, which first dwelt in your grandmother Lois and your mother Eunice, and I'm sure that it is in you as well. (NASB)

Proverbs 1:8 & 10:

> Hear my son, your father's instruction and do not forsake your mother's teaching. Indeed, they are a graceful wreath to your head, **a crown and ornaments about your neck.** (NASB) (Emphasis mine)

1 Thessalonians 2:7-8:

> [7] But we proved to be gentle among you **as a nursing mother tenderly cares for her own children.** [8] Having so fond an affection for you, we were well pleased to impart to you not only the gospel of God, but also our own lives. (NASB) (Emphasis mine)

Stephanie prayed:

Thank you, Lord, for this crown and this mantle that you're reestablishing of how we can receive love from you, from Heaven, and how we can be healed from childhood wounds and chips on our shoulders so that the mantles can fall upon us properly.

Help us to have more understanding about these mantles that come with crowns and the mantles that are on the ground that we need to retrieve.

Give us insight, give us instruction. Open the eyes of our understanding.

Malcolm, thank you.

Now that we know that each crown has a corresponding mantle, we can attach our faith to the reception of not *only* the crown, or the reauthorization of a recovered crown, or the anointing that accompanies that crown and the dominion of it, but also its corresponding mantle. In some cases, the weightiness of some crowns can be explained and attributed to the weightiness of the mantle.

We also now have another arena we must deal with—the possible chip on our shoulder. That chip could be offense or dishonor, among many other things. A definition of this idiom is found in the Merriam-Webster Dictionary:

> *: to have an angry or unpleasant attitude or way of behaving caused by a belief that one has been treated unfairly in the past*[17]

---

[17] Merriam-Webster.com Dictionary, s.v. "have a chip on one's shoulder," accessed February 22, 2025, https://www.merriam-webster.com/dictionary/have%20a%20chip%20on%20one%27s%20shoulder.

Example: He has had a chip on his shoulder ever since he didn't get the promotion he was expecting.

———— ∞ ————

Chapter 23

The Superior Crown of Glory

Stephanie began, "We ask to step into the Library of Revelation to receive further information about crowns and to meet with John." We saw John wearing a birthday crown.

We asked, "Is it your birthday? It is some kind of celebration, something we're supposed to note about?"

"It's a celebratory type of crown. It's a milestone," John explained.

Stephanie replied, "Well, thank you for this. I ask that you help us understand it more, whatever this is." John had the book out that we had been learning from. Stephanie had not seen the dragon in front of her just yet, but the book was on the table. It was the Book of Crowns. As she flipped through the book, another crown popped up with yellow stones.

"We've been talking so much about inferior crowns," John spoke. "How about another Superior Crown?"

"That would be lovely. It has something to do with celebration, doesn't it?"

"The burst of sunlight through the yellow gemstones reflects His glorious glory. In, with, and through this crown are the very celebrations of life."

"It's a Crown of Glory!" Stephanie responded.

John elucidated, "He's the glory and the lifter of your head.[18] Doesn't that sound like a celebration? To understand this crown, you must understand the glory."

"John. I don't know that I understand the glory completely."

He explained, "Its radiance breaks through the darkness. The Crown of Glory is what shows to the spirit realm that you are the salt of the earth. Be crowned with the radiance of His glory. Not everyone receives this crown. <u>It must be acquired.</u> It is indeed in and through sonship. However, **this is relational**.

---

[18] Psalms 3:3: But thou, O LORD, *art* a shield for me; my glory, and the lifter up of mine head. (KJV)

> *There are clouds of glory,*
> *there are realms of glory,*
> *and there are crowns of glory.*

"Each is unique and separate unto itself. He is the glory and lifter of your head.

"As the lifter of our head, He causes our head to be held high, which is needed to wear a crown properly. You must walk upright to have this crown on. You're not carrying the crown when your head is hanging low through despair or defeat.

"The Apostle Paul wore this crown. Through his many persecutions, he learned that each experience produced more significant measures of the Glory of God in his life. Paul did not go hunting for challenging situations; they just seemed to find him. At the same time, he did not run from them either. He endured them and let the glory increase in his life."

Stephanie explained what she experienced, "It's interesting; I saw a picture of Jesus Himself putting this on me. I found it unique that sometimes we can pick up the crowns because of our authority, and sometimes Wisdom may give us a particular crown with pearls in it, and now...

> *Jesus is the one*
> *that gives this crown.*

"I saw Him gently put it on my head, and as He did, He lifted my chin and winked at me with a big smile. Thank you, Jesus."

Those that carry the Crown of Fear cannot carry and walk with this crown.[19]

John explained, "Not because the Father doesn't want them to have it, but because *this Superior Crown cannot be in the presence of the inferior crown.* The two cannot correlate or co-exist. That's why it is so important for you to understand He hasn't given you the spirit of fear. You cannot wear both crowns. Will you allow Him to be the glory and the lifter of your head?"

"We will."

John noted, "That is why this is a celebratory crown."

Stephanie was prompted to read John 3:16:

> *The entire cosmos is the object of God's affection. And he is not about to abandon his creation— the gift of his Son is for mankind to realize their origin in him who mirrors their authentic birth—begotten not of flesh but of the Father. In*

---

[19] Discussed in an upcoming chapter.

this persuasion the life of the ages echoes within the individual and announces that the days of regret and sense of lost-ness are over. (MIRROR)

I added, "Days of regret and loss would cause your head to drop."

"Yes. That's right," Stephanie inserted. "Thank you, John. It's beautiful. We receive this crown."

———— ∞ ————

Chapter 24

The Superior Crown of Starlight

Engaging again with Heaven in the Library of Revelation, Stephanie noticed three beings to her left in the room. She could see feathers falling all around as if someone had just had a pillow fight.

She walked around the table, pushing feathers aside because the book we had seen several times before was before her. She heard the phrase "light as a feather" as she turned the page. The crown she saw was orange in color. It was a beautiful orange. This crown seemed heavier than the others she had witnessed. This was the Crown of Starlight.

She asked for clarification and heard the rhyme, "Star light, star bright, the first star I've seen tonight."

Stephanie knew that she could not yet wear this crown, which was faceted by the bright morning star.

> *It is for the sons who seek*
> *the depth of understanding*
> *of the Father's purpose*
> *and will for the Kingdom.*

It is arrayed in beauty from His Majesty. His majestic and delicate works of craftsmanship are bestowed upon this crown.

> *In this Crown of Starlight*
> *is the understanding*
> *of great mysteries.*

Each stone represents light, and each crown is from a star. It is not from a star that we think of in the cosmos but one whose foundations are from the deep. (Deep calls out to deep.) Those who seek the deep find the light of every star that He has fashioned. The light and the star are in direct correlation with the Kingdom of Heaven. This is no ruse.

With the explanation ended, Stephanie asked, "May I ask who you three are and why you are here?"

The first person stepped forward and had an incredible light on their face. It was a woman, and it was as if her skin glistened. She said, "I am. I walk with Wisdom. I am the Spirit of Ages and of the age to come." She then stopped speaking and stepped back.

Another woman stepped forward dressed in all white with fur around her head. She walks with Purity, but didn't reveal any more about herself than that. We realized she was an angel, and the feathers we had seen were hers. She had something to do with Jesus, the Bright and Morning Star.

She stepped forward and put the cup and bread she was holding on the table.

She said, "I was with Him in the garden. I strengthened Him. I was there when He poured Himself out." Stephanie visualized her as she received every drop that was poured out of Jesus during His time in the garden.

We asked her name, but she said that her name was not important. She ministered divine revelation to Jesus. He was crowned with a Crown of Divine Revelation. She was also an angel. As she spoke, Stephanie could sense great reverence.

Stephanie remarked, "I must be content with what you have given me even though I have and want to know more about who you are. I know you're from His star, and you are a part of His star."

———— ∞ ————

Chapter 25

The Crown of Immortality

The angel was still forward, but the third person, or the third being that Stephanie had sensed in the room, stepped forward. He seemed to be masculine.

He said, "I work with time. Your walk with time is the force of energy." Stephanie had a quick glimpse of a star and energy and what that would look like together as well as time. She realized that the three of them serve this crown, and they said that we live and move and have our being in it.

This crown is one to be desired.

Stephanie expressed her desire to have this crown whenever it was time to have it bestowed.

She cast her eyes back upon this crown, which she realized was a living thing. She could see its movement among the stones as if she were seeing them speak to one another. The angel assigned to the star informed Stephanie that she would help teach her because she had such a love for Jesus. It was an amazing privilege for that angel to be the one to minister to Jesus in the garden.

As the angels stepped back, the book closed. During the engagement, I realized that Ezekiel, the chief angel over LifeSpring, had also been in the Garden of Gethsemane with Jesus. We called him near and asked if he had anything to add to the engagement.

Stephanie described what she saw, "Ezekiel approached. There is still a reverence. I see the picture of Jesus in the garden on His knees."

We asked, "Is there anything he could add to what we have been instructed about so far?"

He showed us that the night in the garden was when that crown was placed upon Jesus' head, and He went from suffering and anguish to a clear understanding.

---

*This crown contains
an immortality.*

It wasn't just the Spirit of Christ that came to Earth, but in this moment, His flesh received immortality, and at His death, His flesh would rise in immortality.

"I just assumed that I was getting the understanding because He was God. He's literally a man in heaven. He was a man here, but His mortal body was raised in immortality," Stephanie commented.

Ezekiel responded, "You see, even Jesus had a choice. He received immortality when He made the decision to go through with the crucifixion when He was strengthened. He could have decided not to do this. We have this record."

Matthew 26:39:

> *He went a little farther and fell on His face, and prayed, saying, 'O My Father, **if it is possible**, let this cup pass from Me; **nevertheless**, not as I will, but as You will.' (Emphasis mine)*

He prayed that twice; see verse 42.

Stephanie envisioned where Jesus was broken, and when this Crown of Immortality was put upon Him, strengthening came to His spirit, and He received life and immortality at that moment. He understood that whatever He would go through, He would indeed be raised. His body was raised a few days later.

Stephanie said, "Jesus, thank you for your decision that day. We look forward to understanding this crown more."

———— ∞ ————

Chapter 26
Crowns & Technologies

As we engaged Heaven, the scene before us was a vast, flat landscape upon which the sun was rising. The opening statement from Heaven was, "The sun is rising on new technologies and advancements for the sons on behalf of the Kingdom of Heaven. These are territorial advancements. There are crowns and thrones, dominions and authority that are purposed in this sun that is rising upon the sons.

Specific technologies are in the crowns.

Purpose and dominion are on the thrones.

"These are technologies, supreme in their kind, that are superior and everlasting. With every new sunrise, there is dominion, technologies, and authority the sons must take.

The crowns are key, and **every** *crown has an associated throne.*

"There is a purpose to the new day, and *you must govern the whispers.*

In governing the whispers with these crowns and technologies, authority, and dominion, you will pull down strongholds—ancient ones.

"*This* is a new day!"

We asked, "What do we need to do?

Malcolm and Einstein appeared as our teachers, and Einstein said, "This is my favorite part of the technologies of Heaven. They have been engrafted into each crown using a very interesting code."

There is an encoding on the crowns specific to that particular crown.

For instance, with the Crown of Sonship, we are to incorporate the technologies of the crown into the words that we speak for the new day, the new dominion, and the new authority we have. There is a formula for each crown. Ask Heaven to help you.

I thank you, Father, for this new day and the Crown of Sonship, with the authority and dominion you have given as sons, and the technologies and the Crown of All Things New.

We bless the Earth with the dominion with which you've given the sons. This is the day the Lord has made; we will rejoice and be glad in it.

We co-labor with the angels and walk in the dominion and the authority with which the crown has given us, and we speak life, not death.

We speak of the dominion and authority of Jesus, who makes all things new, to tear down the strongholds of the enemy, to collaborate with the angels as kings and priests as we celebrate the new day.

We could see Einstein blessing the Earth and showing us this dominion and authority over the Earth,

Thank you, Lord, that you make all things new, even the Earth, this day. Thank you for the technologies of Heaven, the dominion, and the authority that you are giving the sons.

We bless the Earth and its fullness that belongs to you.

I kept thinking that we were going to do something deep, but this is the simplicity of blessing the Earth and our dominion and authority, and it is transpiring while we do this.

Colossians 1:16:

> *Everything that is, begins in him; whether in the heavenly realm or upon the earth, visible or invisible, he is the original blueprint of every order of justice and every level of authority, be it kingdoms or governments, principalities or jurisdictions; the original form of all things were founded by him and created for him. (MIRROR)*

Or,

> *For by Him all things were created that are in heaven and that are on earth, visible and invisible, whether **thrones or dominions** or principalities or powers. All things were created through Him and for Him. (Emphasis mine)*

And...

Colossians 1:20:

> *He initiated the reconciliation of all things to himself. Through the blood of the cross **God restored the original harmony**. His reign of peace now extends to every visible thing upon the earth as well as those invisible things which are in the heavenly realm. (Emphasis mine)*

Blessing the Earth **is** dominion.

When we do so, there is something very transformative about what we do. Still, we can't do it appropriately or conduct this appropriately without the crowns because we must understand the authority we have because of the crowns.

Technologies are upon each crown and are encoded into each crown.

Each crown has a differing coding unique to the wearer.

It is different and unique to each person.

As we follow Heaven's instructions and commands in exercising this dominion and verbally bless the Earth, transformational things will occur.

———— ∞ ————

Chapter 27

The Crown of Kingdom Expansion

As I was journaling, I heard:

Keep pressing in for the crown's revelation. More will be coming. There are specific Superior Crowns that you only know a little of. They are superior in every way to the counterfeits brought forth by hell.

Crowns are forged by obedience. Some crowns are forged by consistently obeying instructions. They are already set aside but will be tailored to the specific son as they press their way into greater depths and expressions of obedience to the Father.

Many assume they will receive a particular crown, not understanding that an act of will can seek after some crowns. You can desire a crown, just as you can desire an office. It is in the pursuit that the present comes.

Because each crown carries with it specific instructions and technologies, the purpose of the technologies is to exercise the domain effectively purposed within the particular crown. Many have thought that Heaven did some things randomly, but Heaven is not random. It is very purposeful. The protocols are guardrails for one to observe as they level the playing field for all who seek the benefits of the crown.

You have long wondered why you seek righteousness (Matthew 6:33) when you are already righteous. You are seeking an expansion of the jurisdiction of righteousness in your own life and upon the Earth. Crowns, in one sense, are about jurisdiction. If one seeks to exercise more jurisdiction, they are seeking righteousness.

Heaven wants the Earth to reflect the heavenly realm in every way. Because mankind does not know what they are seeking when they seek righteousness, they do not know what to do with what they received once it manifested in their realms. For some, it was the gift of property, whether as an outright gift or as an especially good deal. Some rejected it because they did not understand it was about Kingdom expansion.

The more jurisdiction you have, the more the Kingdom of Heaven expands upon the Earth. I want the knowledge of My Glory to cover the

Earth as the waters cover the sea. One spot of water, in some way, touches another. One piece of earth, in some way, touches another piece of the Earth. Understand that some of the expansion of My Kingdom on the Earth will be done in practical ways.

You have looked upon land ownership in the wrong fashion. Land ownership is a physical manifestation of the extension of the Kingdom of God upon the Earth. Abraham operated under the authority of the Crown of Kingdom Expansion. That is why he was not concerned about the land division with Lot. He knew the parameters of the crown he wore. He knew it was only a matter of seed, time, and harvest, and his position would be stronger than Lot's had ever been. When you don't have the Kingdom working for you then you seek natural advantages, but the sons know how to subdue the Earth for the purposes of the Kingdom. Abraham had more than 300 men on the payroll, not including the women and children. He knew about Kingdom expansion.

As you have been told, the act of vocally blessing the Earth is an extension and operation of your dominion upon the Earth. Many have settled for an elementary understanding of these things, but I don't want you or your readers to settle for elementary things. I want them to branch out and begin literally possessing the land. If you have an acre, go after two. If you have 10 acres, go after 20. Watch what I will do as you begin enacting trades with land. Some land you will purchase will be traded for other properties that I have in mind for you. Many don't want the workload, but I have equipped my sons more than they know for the workload that they would carry.

Many talk about the wealth of the sinner being laid up for the just, but they expect it will simply fall into their lap. Some may, but most require the trade of labor and energy which you possess as a son. Don't fall for the tricks and traps of everything being entirely easy. You must press into some of these things to see them manifest. I have things for my sons to do, but they have been timid about pursuing them and have pushed these thoughts down and into the backs of their minds. I'm bringing them up again. I am bringing the desire to walk in greater dominion into your life.

I want my sons to prosper
so they can expand the Kingdom.

Crowns are part of the process, but not all of it. Don't settle for one talent when I have 10 available to you. Never settle.

This crown MUST be sought. It is not merely given. Seek the Kingdom and His righteousness first, and all these things will be added to you. What things? Housing, clothing, provision. The stuff you need to do things with. Because of the lack of seeking, it is never a possibility. If you are not seeing the provision, increase the seeking. All the things you need are added when you seek the Kingdom AND His righteousness.

Many have complained that I failed to fulfill that scripture for them, but that is not the case. What failed was the degree of seeking. Many did not govern the whispers. Some of the whispers were to dissuade you, while others were positive whispers to direct you. For some, I gave instruction in the form of a whisper, and they ignored it because it did not fit their image of themselves, and they refused the provision it was designed to bring. When I instruct concerning a particular vocational choice, I have more in mind than just a temporary fix for one's financial woes. I am training My sons in obedience in every aspect of life.

Some say within themselves, 'That (particular job) is beneath me.' They don't understand that obedience to the instruction of Heaven is never beneath you. It will elevate you given you steward the instruction and situation well. I have spoken so many times to My sons, and they did not heed. They, like Elijah, had to understand that the still small voice is a preferred means of communication with them. It requires you to lean in to hear. I want intimacy from My sons so they can follow every instruction as Heaven gives them to build My Kingdom upon the Earth to be the mighty force I have envisioned.

—.—

The following day, as I journaled, I heard:

Other downloads are forthcoming as I want to both cover and restore some things to My sons. Many have walked far below where they could have been or should have been because of misunderstandings within My Word and incorrect teaching. Much of what has been learned about crowns put it off to a future event, but the future does not help the present. Many crowns have current applications for the sons and need to be implemented. Understanding that dominion is for now, not hundreds of years from now, is crucial. In Psalm 8, you are given dominion. Jesus enforced it before his ascension, and I have not changed My mind. Because Jesus has authority, YOU have authority. Because of that imparted authority, you go and preach. You go and make disciples of ALL nations. You baptize them into the nature of the Father, Son, and Holy Spirit.

Hebrews 2:8:

God's intention was that human life should rule the planet. He subjected everything without exception to his control. Yet, looking at the human race, it does not seem that way at all. (MIRROR)

Understand that because
I have a crown, **you** have a crown.

That's what it means to be coronated.

———— ∞ ————

Chapter 28

The False Crown of Deception

or

Crown of Deceit

(The First Crown)

In the following few chapters, we will introduce what Heaven taught us about false crowns provided by the enemy to bring destruction into people's lives. As a matter of simplification, we have provided them in the order we received them. Interspersed with these revelations, Heaven periodically shared about various Superior Crowns that we can partake of. You have already read about those. The first false crown we learned about is the Crown of Deception. You will recognize that this crown operates in many people's lives. Some people you know wear this crown, but the great news is that we can be free. Let's begin....

With this engagement with Heaven, we went in a direction we had not anticipated. The apostle John began to teach us from Revelation, particularly Revelation 12:3:

> *Then, I witnessed in Heaven another significant event. I saw a large red dragon with seven heads and ten horns, with* **seven crowns on his heads**. *(Emphasis mine) (NLT)*

Stephanie's heart skipped a beat when she saw this vision in the realms of Heaven of the red dragon. What really stood out were the crowns on the dragon's heads.

We knew John had some things to teach us, and we watched as he pointed to the crown on the left with a long stick. He explained that this dragon gives the sons false crowns and this crown was one of deception. He explained how this dragon is stealthier than we could think or imagine and that deception comes in many forms.

Mounted on the crown were stones. Each stone was black or different variations of grey. It was an ugly crown, but each stone represented a form of deception.

John explained that when sons receive a righteous crown, it may have pearls or stones embedded. Not so with these false crowns. This is key for us to know as sons because deception is running rampant on the Earth, and even the elect would be deceived. This is a prized crown that the enemy loves to put on the heads of the sons. Think of it like a game. In this crown, there is a stone of self-righteousness."

All of the "selves" are embedded in this inferior crown: self-righteousness, self-hatred, and self-loathing are together, along with self-idolization, self-importance, and self-justification. John explained that self-justification is lethal.

Some of the "selves" we need to be aware of:[20]

- Self-doubt – Lack of confidence in oneself.
- Self-made – Achieving success without outside help.
- Self-sabotage – Behaviors that hinder one's own success.
- Self-sufficient – Able to provide for oneself without outside help.
- Self-centered – Focused only on oneself, sometimes excessively.
- Self-condemnation – Harsh judgment of oneself.
- Self-contempt – Holding oneself in low regard.
- Self-criticism – Evaluating oneself, often negatively.
- Self-deception – Lying to oneself or ignoring reality.
- Self-defeating – Behaviors or attitudes that hinder one's own success.

---

[20] OpenAI. (2025). ChatGPT (February 25, 2025) ChatGPT 4.0 https://chat.openai.com/chat

- Self-delusion – A false belief in one's own abilities or reality.
- Self-denial – The refusal to indulge in one's own desires.
- Self-deprecation – Modest or critical remarks about oneself.
- Self-destruction – Behaviors that lead to harm or failure.
- Self-disgust – Strong dislike for oneself.
- Self-doubt – Uncertainty about one's abilities.
- Self-driven – Motivated without external pressure.
- Self-harm – Intentional injury to oneself.
- Self-hatred – Intense dislike or contempt for oneself.
- Self-importance – An inflated sense of one's own value.
- Self-indulgence – Giving in excessively to one's desires.
- Self-loathing – Intense dislike for oneself.
- Self-pity – Feeling sorry for oneself.
- Self-reproach – Feeling guilty or critical of oneself.
- Self-righteous – Believing one is morally superior to others.

---

*The Crown of Deception
comes as an illusion
of a good crown, but it is not.*

As sons, we must discern. When this crown is put upon the head of a son, the wrong master is in control. He often experiences "delusions of grandeur."

John explained that this understanding would be a technique for freeing the sons. We knew that we would be presented with people who had this inferior crown.

He added that only the Superior Crowns trump this crown as it is a delusion of grandeur. Many will not want to relinquish this crown until they're honest with themselves and the Father. Many prophets wear this inferior crown. They begin to think they are infallible and are certainly not to be questioned.

We wanted to know how to free people who had found themselves wearing this crown. We knew that repentance and forgiveness would be needed. We asked, "How have the sons been tricked?"

John explained that...

> *The basis of this crown is pride.*

He elucidated that this is a crown a narcissist wears. "Indeed, the deeply broken wear this crown," he said. We will often find it on the heads of those who walk in orphanhood—not knowing their father.

Stephanie queried, "John, I understand that this is not how we are to view broken-hearted people. We certainly need not have delusions of grandeur. Usually, one is extremely broken as a child or something horrible happened to them. How do we minister regarding this because we know we're going to be faced with this? What are the steps in the process?"

He explained that we must walk in humility—not grandiosity. Those wearing this crown have no humility. The sons must walk in humility as peace will be their umpire. Those who wear this crown have no peace. Everyone who wears this crown is looking for acceptance.

We have recently seen this demonstrated in some people's lives. The desire for acceptance makes people susceptible to this crown.

However, when we minister to people with this crown, we must remember that humility is the key.

"How do 'know-it-all's make you feel?" John asked.

I responded that they try to make you feel small, while Stephanie pointed out that they get on her nerves. Know-it-alls are not walking in humility. However, she has been called a know-it-all herself.

Many generations bowed their knee to this dragon, this dragon of pride, and were given great understanding—false wisdom. Again, humility is the key.

Humility is the key.

When working with someone, oftentimes, if they are wearing this inferior crown, they can't see that they need this crown to be removed.

Self-striving is involved. Remember, all the "selves" are embodied in this crown.

This Crown of Deception is an ugly crown.

John explained, "A key to humility is a contrite heart. Contriteness is to show remorse. Many who follow LifeSpring have family members who wear this Crown of Deception. Repentance work is key. The key of humility is vital. The Superior Crown of Love is the exchange. You must have remorse for improper or objectionable behavior. Some scriptures talk about contriteness:

Psalm 34:18:

> *The Lord is near to those who have a broken heart and saves **(deliver)** such as have a contrite spirit. (Emphasis mine)*

Psalm 51:17:

> *The sacrifices of God are a broken spirit, a broken and contrite heart—these, oh God, you will not despise. (NLT)*

Isaiah 57:15:

> *The high and lofty one who lives in eternity, the Holy One, says this: 'I live in the high and holy place with those whose spirits are contrite and humble. I restore the crushed spirit of the humble and revive the courage of those with repentant hearts.' (NLT)*

And then Isaiah 66:2:

> *My hands have made both heaven and earth; they and everything in them are mine. I, the LORD, have spoken! 'I will bless those who have humble and contrite hearts, who tremble at my word.' (NLT)*

Matthew 5:3:

> *Blessed are the poor in spirit, for theirs is the Kingdom of Heaven.*

"Those that come to you are looking for answers. You must address the pride. If you don't have a fear of the Lord operating in your life, you will gladly wear these false crowns. The enemy would love to give you these crowns. Remember that the enemy is all about providing false solutions in our lives."

A rejection of truth on any level can set you up to receive a false Crown of Deceit.

How to bring people to freedom who have found themselves wearing this crown:

- The sons must walk in humility—not grandiosity as peace will be their umpire. Humility is the key.
- Repentance and forgiveness need to come.
- As sons, we must discern.
- When you see someone experiencing delusions of grandeur, look for this crown.
- Only the Superior Crowns trump this crown as it is a delusion of grandeur.
- The key of humility is vital.
- A key to humility is a contrite heart. Contriteness is to show remorse.
- Repentance work is key.
- The Superior Crown of Love is the exchange.
- You must have remorse for improper or objectionable behavior.
- You must address the pride.
- You must have a fear of the Lord operating in your life.

Removing a False Crown

1. Repent for embracing the Crown of Deception out of your brokenness, arrogance, and pride.
2. Repent for every vestige of pride, arrogance, or brokenness in your own life.
3. Remove the false crown from your head.

4. Ask for the Crown of Humility in its place, as well as the Crown of Righteousness.

Generational False Crowns

Sometimes, these false crowns will be passed from generation to generation. You want that false crown removed from your generational line. Repent for those in your generational line who embraced the Crown of Deceit out of their brokenness, arrogance, and pride. Repent for any vestiges of pride, arrogance, or brokenness in your own life. Remove the inferior crown from your head and the crown on your generational line and ask for the Crown of Humility in its place *and* a Crown of Righteousness.

Removal of a Generational False Crown

1. Repent for those in your generational line who embraced the Crown of Deceit out of their brokenness, arrogance, and pride.
2. Repent for any vestiges of pride, arrogance, or brokenness in your own life.
3. Remove the crown from your head and the crown on your generational line.
4. Ask for the Crown of Humility in its place, as well as the Crown of Righteousness.

Remember, humility provides protection from these false crowns. As Psalm 100:3 says:

Know that the LORD, He is God; **it is He who has made us, and not we ourselves;** *we are His people and the sheep of His pasture. (Emphasis mine)*

Prayer for the Removal of the False Crown of Deception

Father, we ask to enter the realms of Heaven through Jesus. We invite the Seven Spirits of God, the angels, and our cloud of witnesses. We ask to enter the Court of Mercy.

We request that You bring into this Court everyone in our generations, both mother and father's side, as well as those related to us by blood, marriage, adoption, civil or religious covenants, all the way to Your hand in the Garden and all the way forward as far as it needs to go.

We request that the accuser of the brethren be brought into this Court. Your Honor, we agree with the adversary that we and our generations have picked up this false Crown of Deception through pride, arrogance, lies, delusions of grandeur, false humility, and through all of the selves. We repent for every self-deception that we have accepted and traded with. We repent for self-idolization, and we repent where we have been unteachable. We repent for self-promotion and self-striving instead of being led by Holy Spirit.

Father, we repent for deceiving others and for allowing this crown to rest upon their heads. We agree with the adversary that we have all been guilty of this. We repent for allowing the false mantle to fall and where we were glad to wear it proudly.

We repent for hearing Your voice speaking to us to remove it, and instead, we agreed to hang onto it tightly. We repent for not taking the keys of the Kingdom of Heaven and closing these doors, realms, gates, and bridges. We repent where you've allowed us to use the key of humility to close these doors forever, and instead, we rebelled. We repent for the dishonor we brought upon ourselves, others, and you, Lord, for wearing this Crown of Deception, agreeing with delusions of grandeur, and thinking of ourselves more highly than we ought to.

We repent for being distracted by this Crown of Deception and allowing its deception to bring us further and further and further away from the truth. We repent for being awestruck with the illusion of this crown. We repent for the throne, which is the altar of worship, where we have worshipped ourselves, worshipped what we've accomplished, and even worshipped the pain in our thoughts and minds.

We ask that the angels come and take this altar, this throne, and the idols upon it, which are all of our selfs. We repent for the use of this crown as well as every gray and black stone representing the selfs. We repent for where we have pride and present the crown, the throne, and the mantle to this court for judgment.

We ask that the angels bring every spirit associated with and assigned to this crown into the court for judgment. We turn now to our generations, and we forgive, bless, and release you for participating with this crown. We forgive you for perpetuating it through the generations and for placing it upon the heads of others and WE repent for where WE have placed it upon the heads of others as well. We ask for the blood of Jesus. We ask for the full destruction of the crown, the throne, and the mantle.

We request that the stain of this crown that was left upon the heads of the sons be removed by the blood of Jesus, and we ask that it become white as snow. We request the mantels be rent in two and torn as we bow in this court before the Just Judge of the Universe. We bow in humility. We say, 'Have mercy on us, Jesus. We ask that you walk through the timeline in our generations. Please deliver to us Your Crown of Righteousness. We agree that we have strayed because of these false, inferior crowns. We ask that you take our hand and bring our generations back to the truth. We ask for mercy and your righteous verdict on our behalf and those of our generations.

We receive your righteous verdict or further counsel, Your Honor.

[If further counsel is advised, follow these instructions. Once you have received a righteous verdict, begin the following segment:]

With our righteous verdict in hand, we speak to the Earth. We speak to you that every one of our generations who stepped upon you, even those related to us by blood, marriage, adoption, civil or religious covenant.

Earth, we have received a righteous verdict from the Courts of Heaven this day. We bless you to hear the word of the Lord. We bless you to swallow up the iniquity and the egregious sins of self-deception and wearing these crowns. Swallow up every word and deed that was done upon you. Swallow the innocent bloodshed, sexual sins, moving of the boundary stones, worship of ourselves, idol worship, occultic worship, theft—every sin under the sun that Jesus died for. We charge you to swallow it up and bless you to your original design. We bless you to see the governing sons and to begin blessing us. Begin pouring out your riches of abundance of truth and life.

We request the blood of Jesus to cover every place this was done upon you or in you. We speak to the frequencies of the wind to blow away the evil, to the water to drown it, and to the fire to burn it. We speak to you to return to your original design as the Lord had created you. The Earth is the Lord's, and its fullness belongs to the Lord.

We speak peace. We thank the Just Judge. We thank you, Jesus, the author and the finisher of our faith, for the Crowns of Righteousness and the Crown of Love that trump this inferior crown.

As governing sons, we pick up these Superior Crowns, place them upon our heads, and ask you to help us rule. We commission the angels to render these righteous verdicts in the spirit and the natural. We commission the angels to put this on record.

As a son, we call in the treasure that has been lost from the north, the south, the east, and the west in every age, realm, dimension, and time to fill the capacity of this section.

Thank you, Just Judge, for honoring us and trusting us with the responsibility of wearing these Crowns of Love and Righteousness. Thank you for helping us occupy the territory you assigned us. We don't take this lightly and we ask for supernatural assistance and help daily to govern well as your sons, in the name of Jesus.

We ask that all of this be done in time and out of time, and in every age, realm, and dimension, and that all of the spiritual debris, residue, and essences that were left behind by this inferior crown and the spirits that came with it be destroyed utterly. We thank you, Father, for what you did, Jesus, for giving us authority and dominion here.

Characteristics of the False Crown of Deception

- The Crown of Deceit is ugly.
- Each stone on the crown represents a form of deception.
- Because deception is running rampant on the Earth, even the elect would be deceived.

- This is a prized crown that the enemy loves to put on the heads of the sons.
- In this crown, there is a stone of self-righteousness.
- All the "selves" are in this crown: self-righteousness, self-hatred, and self-loathing are together, along with self-idolization, self-importance, and self-justification.
- Self-striving is involved.
- Self-justification is lethal.
- The Crown of Deceit is an illusion of a good crown, but it is not.
- When this crown is put upon the head of a son, the master is in control. He often experiences "delusions of grandeur."
- Many will not want to relinquish this crown until they are honest with themselves and the Father.
- Many prophets wear this crown. They begin to think they are infallible and are certainly not to be questioned.
- The basis of this crown is pride.
- This is a crown a narcissist wears.
- Only the deeply broken wear this crown.
- Often, you find it on the heads of those who are orphans.
- Everyone who wears this crown is looking for acceptance.
- The desire for acceptance drives people to be susceptible to this crown.

- Many who follow LifeSpring have family members who wear this Crown of Deceit.
- Those wearing this crown have no humility.
- If you don't have a fear of the Lord operating in your life, you will gladly wear this false crown.
- The enemy would love to give you this crown.
- Remember that the enemy is all about providing false solutions in your life.
- A rejection of truth on any level can set you up to receive a false Crown of Deceit.

———— ∞ ————

Chapter 29
The False Crown of Loathing
(The Third Crown)

As we engaged with Heaven in the Library of Revelation, Stephanie was again seeing the image of the red dragon. The apostle John appeared and remarked, "Back for more, huh?"

"Of course!"

He began, "Today, we are going to discuss the third crown, which is the Crown of Loathing. It is a great Crown of Wickedness. This is the third crown on the dragon's head.

"What do you think loathing is?" He asked us.

To loathe something is to deeply hate it. It is the epitome of hatred to hate something. You must go deep to the core of this injustice. This crown *sits with injustice*. It mandates the wickedness of injustice. This crown is the blackest of black, void of light, void of truth.

Satan wears this crown as he loathes God.

John explained, "His hatred for the Father is so deep that he will do anything to hurt Him. To kill, steal, and destroy from the sons deeply wounds the Father. This stems from loathing not only God but also the sons—His created ones.

"Loathing has a stench to it, as does this crown. There is darkness, but a sense of belonging comes with this crown. The belief system to loathe something so deeply gives a sense of belonging that is false and in great error in every manner.

"With this crown comes a throne, a seat of wickedness and iniquity, and those that sit upon it sit in darkness not only in this life but in the next.

"What does the Word say about hatred? Hatred is vile. What is the opposite of hatred? Love. Hatred is devoid of love. This crown loathes love and anything that love brings."

Stephanie interjected, "John, I see this head of this dragon with this Crown of Loathing on it. From the head of this one, the mouth is opening, and fire is coming from it."

"Hatred consumes. It consumes the innocent," John explained. "There are aspects of loathing and hatred that consume even other dark entities. It is ferocious. Its appetite is big. The sons must grapple with hatred against God and man in their hearts.

*Do not accept this crown
or sit on its throne.*

*It will eat you alive
and consume you.*

"It is utter darkness. That's why you must be careful with your heart.

*The root of bitterness
is the beginning of this crown
being placed.*

"The beginning of bitterness is offense, which generally starts when we do not govern the whisperings and innuendos. Let love be the ending. Desire the fruits of the spirit."

We noticed that he suddenly turned to leave, so we asked, "Are you leaving? We saw you turn to leave."

"There isn't anything else to say about this crown. Jesus died so that no one should wear this crown, and yet many do. Stephanie, with what Jesus did for us, we should never wear this crown," he concluded.

She remarked, "What's interesting is that John said this crown has a throne that we sit on, too. What is even more interesting is that some people who wear this feel accepted—there's a false acceptance. I would imagine it has to do with pride or feeling like I don't have to love anybody or anything. I can only love myself."

1 John 4:20-21:

> [20] *If someone says, 'I love God,' and* **hates his brother**, *he is a liar; for he who does not love his brother whom he has seen, how can he love God whom he has not seen?* [21] *And this commandment we have from Him: that he who loves God must love his brother also. (Emphasis mine)*

1 John 3:15:

> *Whoever* **hates his brother** *is a murderer, and you know that no murderer has eternal life abiding in him. (Emphasis mine)*

Proverbs 26:24-28:

> [24] *He who* **hates**, *disguises it with his lips, and lays up deceit within himself.* [25] *When he speaks kindly, do not believe him, for there are* **seven abominations in his heart;** [26] *though his* **hatred is covered by deceit**, *his wickedness will be revealed before the assembly.*

²⁷ Whoever digs a pit will fall into it, and he who rolls a stone will have it roll back on him.

*²⁸ A lying tongue **hates** those who are crushed by it, and a flattering mouth works ruin. (Emphasis mine)*

Removal of the Crown of Loathing

1. Repent for embracing the Crown of Loathing out of hatred and the root of bitterness.
2. Repent for embracing offense.
3. Repent for every vestige of hatred, disrespect, dishonor, and lying in your own life.
4. Remove the false crown from your head.
5. Ask for the Crown of Love.

Prayer for Removal of the Crown of Loathing

Father, we ask to step into the Court of Mercy to receive mercy in our time of need. We request the accuser of the brethren be brought in as well as our generations, those related to us by blood, marriage, adoption, civil or religious covenant, all the way to Your hand in the garden and back to Your hand.

We come to you, and we repent for embracing the Crown of Loathing out of hatred and the root of bitterness. We repent for embracing offense, and we repent for every vestige of hatred, disrespect, dishonor, and lying in our own lives.

We repent where we have ever loathed anyone or anything in our generations; we repent. We repent where we have allowed, agreed with, or perpetuated the spirit of antichrist, but also where those who are or were anti-God, where we allowed this inferior crown to bring an atheistic mentality. We repent for cooperation with that. We repent for our hatred of the Father and those who are His. We repent for engaging in the stench of these sins. We repent for sitting in a league with injustice, promoting injustice, and being unjust. We repent for mandating the wickedness of injustice.

We repent for being void of truth. We repent for agreeing with, being a part of, and loving the sense of belonging by wearing this inferior crown. We repent for sitting on the throne of loathing with its seat of wickedness and iniquity. We repent for the great error of wearing this crown. We repent for believing the false acceptance, the pride, and the belief that we do not have to love you or anyone else, only ourselves. Please forgive us. We repent for loathing love. We repent for not accepting your love and for not loving others or even ourselves.

Father, forgive us and our generations, those who were atheists, those who loathed the Word of God, the truth around it, and those who had bitterness in their hearts; we repent. We repent for the utter hatred of anything that presented itself from you or from others that were or carried the embodiment of Your love or what it would bring. We repent for having an appetite for loathing and for hating you, God and man.

We ask for the angels to go through time, on behalf of ourselves and our generations, to remove the crowns of loathing and destroy them.

We ask the angels to remove the Crowns of Loathing placed upon our family's heads, of those who don't trust or believe, for it came from an iniquitous generation. We ask that the throne be destroyed, the seat of wickedness be destroyed, and iniquity be forever vanquished, banished, and removed forevermore from us and our generations. We repent for being a part of consuming the innocent and taking innocence away from others because of wearing this inferior crown. We repent for being a part of others losing their Superior Crowns, where we removed them, or where their crowns became lost.

Jesus, we ask for your blood to cover us and for those crowns to be removed from our children, our grandchildren, our mothers, our fathers, our sisters, our brothers, our friends, and our neighbors. We speak that it must bow to the Superior Crown of King Jesus and the crowns we wear—The Crown of Sonship and the Crown of Love, in Jesus' name.

Righteous Judge, we ask for your verdict or further counsel.

[If further counsel is advised, follow these instructions. Once you have received a righteous verdict, begin the following segment:]

We speak to the Earth that every one of our generations stepped upon, even those related to us by blood, marriage, adoption, civil or religious covenant.

Earth, we have received a righteous verdict from the Courts of Heaven this day. We bless you to hear the word of the Lord. We bless you to swallow up the iniquity and the egregious sins of self-deception and wearing these inferior crowns. Swallow up every word and deed that was done upon you. Swallow the innocent bloodshed, sexual sins, moving of the boundary stones, worship of ourselves, idol worship, occultic worship, theft—every sin under the sun that Jesus died for. We charge you to swallow it up and bless you to your original design. We bless you to see the governing sons and to begin blessing us. Begin pouring out your riches of abundance of truth and life.

We request the blood of Jesus to cover every place this was done upon you or in you. We speak to the frequencies of the wind to blow away the evil, to the water to drown it, and to the fire to burn it. We speak to you to return to your original design as the Lord had created you. The Earth is the Lord's, and its fullness belongs to the Lord.

We speak peace. We thank the Just Judge. We thank you, Jesus, the author and the finisher of our faith, for the Crowns of Righteousness and the Crown of Love that trump this inferior crown.

As governing sons, we pick up these Superior Crowns, place them upon our heads, and ask you to help us rule.

We commission the angels to render these righteous verdicts in the spirit and the natural. We commission the angels to put this on record.

Thank you, Just Judge, for honoring us and trusting us with the responsibility of wearing these Crowns of Love and Righteousness. Thank you for helping us occupy the territory you assigned us. We don't take this lightly and ask for supernatural assistance and help daily to govern well as your sons, in the name of Jesus.

As a son, we call in the treasure that has been lost from the north, the south, the east, and the west in every age, realm, dimension, and time to fill the capacity of this section.

Thank you, Just Judge, for honoring us and trusting us with the responsibility of wearing these Crowns of Love and Righteousness. Thank you for helping us occupy the territory you assigned us. We don't take this lightly and we ask for supernatural assistance and help daily to govern well as your sons, in the name of Jesus.

We ask that all of this be done in time and out of time, and in every age, realm, and dimension, and that all of the spiritual debris, residue, and essences that were left behind by this inferior crown and the spirits that came with it be destroyed utterly. We thank you, Father, for what you did, Jesus, for giving us authority and dominion here.

Characteristics of the Crown of Loathing

- It is a great Crown of Wickedness.
- The third crown on the dragon's head.
- To loathe something is to hate it intensely.
- It is the epitome of hatred to hate something.
- This crown is the blackest of black, void of light, void of truth.
- Satan wears this crown as he loathes God.
- This crown sits with injustice.
- It mandates the wickedness of injustice.
- Satan's hatred for the Father is so deep that he will do anything to hurt Him. To kill, steal, and destroy from the sons deeply wounds the Father. This stems from loathing not only God but also the sons—His created ones.
- Loathing has a stench to it, as does this crown.
- There is darkness, but a sense of belonging comes with this crown.
- The belief system to loathe something so deeply gives a sense of belonging that is false and in great error in every manner.
- With this crown comes a throne, a seat of wickedness and iniquity.
- Those that sit upon sit, not only darkness in this life but in the next.
- Hatred is devoid of love.
- This crown loathes love and anything that love brings.
- Hatred consumes. It consumes the innocent.

- There are aspects of loathing and hatred that consume even other dark entities.
- It is ferocious.
- Its appetite is big.
- The sons must grapple with hatred in their hearts against God and against man.
- Do not accept this crown or sit on its throne.
- It will eat you alive and consume you.
- It is utter darkness.
- That's why you have to be careful with your heart.
- The root of bitterness is the beginning of this.
- The beginning of bitterness is offense.
- That generally starts when we do not govern the whisperings and innuendos. Let love be the ending. Desire the fruits of the spirit.
- Jesus died so that no one should wear this crown, and yet many do.
- You must go deep to the core of this injustice.

———— ∞ ————

Chapter 30

The False Crown of Fear

(The Second Crown)

We asked to step into the Library of Revelation as we wanted to know more about the second crown.

John the apostle was with us again, so we asked him, "What is it you want to teach us about the crowns on this dragon's head?"

John took Stephanie around to the back of the picture she was seeing. She saw a crown from the back which had what appeared to be an open door.

"What does this mean?" we asked.

He said, "This crown is superior in its inferiority. It is the Crown of Fear."

He showed us that when this crown (which is on many people) is placed on someone's head, many demonic entities come with it and are then released into the person's life. Picture how they may come in from the back door mentioned above.

> *It is a release of the essence of each of them because with fear comes a lot of other negative things.*

When this Crown of Fear is placed upon a person, it will open up a throne, and all these negative things will begin pouring out, encircling their head and trying to manifest around, in, and through their mind.

2 Timothy 1:7:

> *For God has not given us a spirit of fear, but of power and of love and of a sound mind.*

The Lord said, "I have not given you a spirit of fear, which is a specific dark entity, but with the spirit of fear comes the Crown of Fear, and the enemy distributes this crown to many."

> *Wearing this crown brings a distortion to the mind and even affects the heart.*

This crown rules over many of the other inferior crowns, so that's superior to the inferior crowns.

Many people have this crown thrust upon them through traumas. When you have trouble receiving from Heaven, there may be fear coming from the generations. You may have to remove the Crown of Fear from your head continually.

How do we do this where we don't accept it ever again? The head of this dragon is a master manipulator. This crown creates a stronghold, and when this crown is put on the heads of the sons, it is as if it tries to become embedded in them. It doesn't just sit on the head; it digs into the person's head to pierce it.

Of course, we don't want anything to do with this crown and its ability to distort our ability to receive and flow in revelation. As governing sons, that should make us mad.

Prayer for Removal of the Crown of Fear

Lord, we ask to step into Your Court of Mercy to receive mercy in our time of need. We ask that our generations be brought into this Court and those related to us by blood, marriage, adoption, civil or religious covenant, to Your hand in the garden and forward as far as it needs to go.

Lord, I present to you ourselves and our generations, and every one of us who ever wore this inferior crown, who willingly took this Crown of Fear, who even distributed it to other people in our family and our generations, and even those outside of our generations where we instilled fear, where we presented fear, where we were a part of fear, where we perpetuated fear throughout the generational line, or where we have accepted it, bent our knee to it, or even relished in it, or relished in it in others. Forgive us, Lord; we repent. I ask for the blood of Jesus to be applied to this.

We are requesting that this inferior crown be removed from me and our generational line as it pierced our heads. We ask that the angels remove this crown, even though it is not easily taken off, along with every binding and every structure that would keep it upon the heads of the sons, that the crown be taken off and destroyed.

We ask that the Superior Crown of Love be placed upon our heads to heal any woundedness and begin to mend our minds and mend the places of woundedness.

We ask that the technology of the Crowns of Sonship that we wear and the new day would infiltrate and destroy the technology of the Crown of Fear and that the nanotechnology of Jesus—of His love (for He has not given us the spirit of fear, but of power) and that the power and the dominion of the Superior Crown crush and destroy the inferior Crown of Fear.

Father has not given us the spirit of fear but of love, and that love is the Supreme Crown over this inferior crown, and as the Crown of a Sound Mind is placed upon our heads, that it heals every wound of the mind and that the poison that came with that inferior Crown of Fear be drawn up out of us as we are made new.

We commission the angels to clean up the spiritual debris, residue, and essences that the spirit of fear has left behind, and we receive the Crown of Superiority from Jesus, the Crown of Love, the Crown of Power, the dominion over this, and the Crown of a Sound Mind. Thank you, Lord.

We come out of agreement with every superiority of this inferior crown. We are not in agreement with it. Where we and our generations agreed, and where we were lied to, and we believed that there was not anything we could do because we were so gripped by fear; that is a lie. We come out of agreement with the lie of this inferior Crown of Fear. We ask for the cancellation and annulment of these lies.

We commission the angels to capture every demonic spirit that came with the spirit of fear that came through the back door of this crown.

(What it did was open the door to other spirits.)

We commission the angels to gather up these spirits and take them to be judged—those that infiltrated the mind and the heart, those that brought the lies and instilled the fear.

Lord, we ask in the Courts of Heaven that these inferior spirits be judged on behalf of the sons. We receive your righteous verdicts on behalf of us and our generations.

We ask that these inferior crowns be destroyed. Thank you for the Crown of a New Day—of your new for us. Thank you for the Superior Crown of the mind of Christ and the Crown of Love. Thank you, Jesus. I ask Father for the healing balm for the wounds. When this inferior Crown of Fear is placed on people's heads, it creates ugly wounds.

Further, we request the destruction of this throne, mantle and crown by the name and blood of Jesus.

We come out of agreement with the master of this crown. Forgive us where we traded and agreed with it.

Your Honor, we ask for your righteous verdict or further counsel.

[If further counsel is advised, follow these instructions. Once you have received a righteous verdict, begin the following segment:]

We speak to the Earth that every one of our generations stepped upon, even those related to us by blood, marriage, adoption, civil or religious covenant.

Earth, we have received a righteous verdict from the Courts of Heaven this day. We bless you to hear the word of the Lord. We bless you to swallow up the iniquity and the egregious sins of self-deception and wearing these inferior crowns. Swallow up every word and deed that was done upon you. Swallow the innocent bloodshed, sexual sins, moving of the boundary stones, worship of ourselves, idol worship, occultic worship, theft—every sin under the sun that Jesus died for. We charge you to swallow it up and bless you to your original design. We bless you to see the governing sons and to begin blessing us. Begin pouring out your riches of abundance of truth and life.

We request the blood of Jesus to cover every place this was done upon you or in you. We speak to the frequencies of the wind to blow away the evil, to the water to drown it, and to the fire to burn it. We speak to you to return to your original design as the Lord had created you. The Earth is the Lord's, and its fullness belongs to the Lord.

We speak peace. We thank the Just Judge. We thank you, Jesus, the author and the finisher of our faith, for the Crowns of Righteousness and the Crown of Love that trump this inferior crown.

As governing sons, we pick up these Superior Crowns, place them upon our heads, and ask you to help us rule. We commission the angels to render these righteous verdicts in the spirit and the natural. We commission the angels to put this on record.

Thank you, Just Judge, for honoring us and trusting us with the responsibility of wearing these Crowns of Love and Crowns of Righteousness. Thank you for helping us occupy the territory you assigned us. We don't take this lightly; ask for supernatural assistance and help daily to govern as well as your sons in the name of Jesus.

As a son, we call in the treasure that has been lost from the north, the south, the east, and the west in every age, realm, dimension, and time to fill the capacity of this section.

We ask that all of this be done in time and out of time, and in every age, realm, and dimension, and that all of the spiritual debris, residue, and essences that were left behind by this inferior crown and the spirits that came with it be destroyed utterly. We thank you, Father, for what you did, Jesus, for giving us authority and dominion here.

Characteristics of the False Crown of Fear

- This crown is superior in its inferiority.
- When this crown (which is on many people) is placed on someone's head, many demonic entities come with this crown. They are released into the person's life.
- It is a release of the essence of each of them because with fear comes many other negative things.
- When this Crown of Fear is placed upon a person, it will open a throne, and negative things will begin pouring out and encircling their head and trying to manifest in their mind.
- With the spirit of fear comes these Crowns of Fear, and the enemy distributes these crowns.
- Wearing this crown brings a distortion to the mind and even affects the heart.

- This crown rules over many of the other inferior crowns, so that's superior to the inferior crowns.
- Many people have this crown thrust upon them through traumas.
- When you have trouble receiving from Heaven, there may be fear coming from your generations.
- You may have to remove the Crown of Fear from your head continually.
- This particular head of this dragon is a master manipulator.
- This crown creates a stronghold.
- When this crown is put on the heads of the sons, it is as if it tries to become embedded in them. It doesn't just sit on the head; it digs into the person's head to pierce it.
- This crown distorts your ability to receive and flow in revelation. As a governing son, that should make you mad.

———— ∞ ————

Chapter 31
The False Crown of Devouring
(The Seventh Crown)

We accessed the Library of Revelation to learn more about the false crowns, and John beckoned Stephanie to sit down. As she sat down, her chair turned, and the bookcase on the wall opened like doors. She could see only the middle head of the dragon. The entire neck and head of the dragon were on fire. It was fierce looking. John said, "Notice the downward thrust of the head of the dragon.

"This dragon uses a thrust."

Stephanie replied, "Is it that this crown is thrust upon the sons or because I see it as a motion, as his head is down and thrust upwards? That would seem to me to elevate someone."

John then gave her a bird's eye view of the crown on someone's head. She could see that at the back of the crown were two gems mounted higher than the other gems on the crown—almost making them appear like horns. It gave this dragon the appearance of having horns. There was a combination of red and black stones together on the crown. John called it the *Crown of Devouring*. It is the seventh false crown. She noticed that the black and red colors of the stones seemed to play off one another, with the red reminding Stephanie of fire that would devour.[21]

John explained that the head of this crown was seeking whom he may devour. Stephanie could see the dragon with his head lowered to the ground like he was sniffing something out. He is sniffing out the weak, sniffing out those on the edge, and seeking whom he can devour. This part of the head of the dragon with this crown *hunts after the sons*. It's a fierce crown. This is a fierce crown in league with the sons of perdition—the ones that have given themselves over to darkness, also referred to as Sons of Belial or S.O.B's.

He asked us, "Did you know sin leaves a stench? You have heard that this part of the dragon hunts with this crown. With this stench, he can smell you."

---

[21] 1 Peter 5:8: Be sober, be vigilant; because your adversary the devil walks about like a roaring lion, seeking whom he may devour.

"That's terrifying, John. It's so terrifying to see this crown's horn-like feature and the flames around it," Stephanie answered.

Jude 1:17-23:

> *^{17} But you, beloved, remember the words which were spoken before by the apostles of our Lord Jesus Christ: ^{18} how they told you that there would be mockers in the last time who would walk according to their own ungodly lusts. ^{19} These are sensual persons, who cause divisions, not having the Spirit.*
>
> *^{20} But you, beloved, building yourselves up on your most holy faith, praying in the Holy Spirit, ^{21} keep yourselves in the love of God, looking for the mercy of our Lord Jesus Christ unto eternal life. ^{22} And on some have compassion, making a distinction; ^{23} but others save with fear, pulling them out of the fire, **hating even the garment defiled by the flesh.** (Emphasis mine)*

John continued, "There are those *that follow darkness,* and there are those *that fall into darkness.* There is a difference. This dragon hunts both. He has many crowns, and he seeks to devour. Most don't return when this crown is put upon their head. It's lethal. That's what devouring does."

"I always think of the goodness of God being able to offer recompense to the lost," Stephanie interjected.

John asked, "What is devouring?"

"I look at it as a consuming, but you tell me."

"Is there ever anything left when fire devours?"

"Not really. The charred remains only."

"With this crown, you lose all sensibility and sense of oneness," John explained. "The most hardened of hearts wear this crown; this isn't just the atheistic view; this is <u>a hatred of God</u>, a turning away, and the true son of perdition. It's not like the average sinner wears this crown, but this dragon seeks to devour common sense and commonalities in people's lives to be able to hear the voice of God, as well as see God. That is what this dragon is after—to devour truth. The darkest of the dark wear this crown."

It's not the average atheist or sinner who wears this crown. This is like the deepest, darkest, blackest-hearted people—the ones that consume babies and murder and are on a path of what we would call the evil ones. An example would be Adolf Hitler or some of his assistants. It is sniffing out sin.

It works in tandem with all other crowns because it seeks to devour. The visual was of a devoured person, as if someone had been in a fire, and there was nothing left but the charred remains. It reminded Stephanie of Pompeii. Instead of white ash, it was black.

I asked, "Is there a scripture John can point us to?"

2 Thessalonians 2:3:

*Let no one deceive you by any means; for that Day will not come unless the falling away comes first, and the man of sin is revealed, the **son of perdition**. (Emphasis mine)*

John 17:12:

*While I was with them in the world, I kept them in Your name. Those whom You gave Me I have kept; and none of them is lost except **the son of perdition**, that the Scripture might be fulfilled. (Emphasis mine)*

---

*There is no light in them.
There is only darkness.*

John pointed to the three crowns we had learned about up to this point: The Crown of Deceit, the Crown of Loathing, and the Crown of Fear. Knowledge about further crowns was forthcoming.

Stephanie noted, "I see images, awful images, of these people that are eating flesh. It's awful looking. I see them eating flesh, and blood is dripping from their mouths."

I added that "perdition" usually means perishing, lostness, dying, or destruction.

She noted, "That would be if they have no light in them. These are the ones that he is seeking, whom he can devour and take to hell with him. This is the ugliest head of a dragon that I've seen. It has all the fire. One head had fire coming out of its mouth. This one has fire naturally coming off the neck and head, and I can see it sniffing people out. When you sin, it begins sniffing you out."

He is roaming about and seeking to devour things. He has been looking for the crowns. The roaming is about looking for those whose crown he can steal.

Stephanie asked John, "What would you want us to know about bringing freedom to someone in this situation?"

He replied, "The other crowns must be removed before this one is addressed. I wanted you to see the end from the beginning."

"We don't need to get ahead of ourselves, do we, John? It comforts me that there is so much hope for those who are lost and deceived. The atheists and those family members who don't believe they are wearing this crown, but they are. They have purposefully stepped over into something really dark. *They have no conscience.* I think serial killers probably wear this crown."

Prayer for Removal of a Crown of Devouring

[Repentance for this crown needs to follow repentance for all the other crowns.]

Father, we ask to step into Your Court of Mercy to receive mercy in our time of need. We ask that the accuser of the brethren be brought into this court as well as our generations, those related to us by blood, marriage, civil and religious covenant, all the way back to Your hand in the garden and all the way forward to Your hand.

Your Honor, this Crown of Devouring cannot be removed until the other crowns are removed. However, we would like to begin the court case process today.

Your Honor, we repent for ourselves and our generations for partnering, agreeing with, and participating with the darkest of the darkest of sins. We repent that we put ourselves and our generations in danger of being hunted because of these sins. We repent for our weaknesses in not seeking after God. We repent for our generations' sins that created a stench that the enemy could sniff out.

We repent for living on the edge, allowing this dragon to hunt us and those in our generations. We repent for being in league with the sons of perdition—the ones that have given themselves over to darkness. We repent for losing all sensibility and sense of oneness of our spirit, soul and body in cooperation with the Lord. We repent for becoming and having the most hardened of hearts. We repent for having stepped over into something dark purposefully and for agreeing to have no conscience.

We repent for allowing ourselves to be void of truth. We repent for taking up the other crowns and then wearing this one—the last. We repent for the lust of blood, the drinking of blood, and the eating of flesh from the kingdom of darkness. We are only to take in the blood and body of Christ. We repent for ourselves and our generations. We repent for the idea of getting near the unholy fire and letting it burn us and for basking in it, allowing it to consume us.

We request that all crowns be destroyed and that this specific crown be fully removed and destroyed, as we have done the repentance work. We request the full removal of this vile crown from our heads as well as from the heads of our generations. We ask that it be burned in the Holy Fire of the Lord God Almighty.

We request the amendment of 'As if it Never Were' and ask for restoration in the mighty name of Jesus.

Please burn the spiritual residue, essences, and debris. In Jesus' name, we ask for the Superior Crowns of the Kingdom of Heaven to be placed on our heads, overturning the egregiousness of our sins.

We ask for your righteous verdict, your honor or further counsel.

[If further counsel is advised, follow these instructions. Once you have received a righteous verdict, begin the following segment:]

We speak to the Earth that every one of our generations stepped upon, even those related to us by blood, marriage, adoption, civil or religious covenant.

Earth, we have received a righteous verdict from the Courts of Heaven this day. We bless you to hear the word of the Lord. We bless you to swallow up the iniquity and the egregious sins of self-deception and wearing these crowns. Swallow up every word and deed that was done upon you. Swallow the innocent bloodshed, sexual sins, moving of the boundary stones, worship of ourselves, idol worship, occultic worship, theft—every sin under the sun that Jesus died for. We charge you to swallow it up and bless you to your original design. We bless you to see the governing sons and to begin blessing us. Begin pouring out your riches of abundance of truth and life.

We request the blood of Jesus to cover every place this was done upon you or in you. We speak to the frequencies of the wind to blow away the evil, to the water to drown it, and to the fire to burn it. We speak to you to return to your original design as the Lord had created you. The Earth is the Lord's, and its fullness belongs to the Lord.

We speak peace. We thank the Just Judge. We thank you, Jesus, the author and the finisher of our faith, for the Crowns of Righteousness and the Crown of Love that trump this inferior crown.

As governing sons, we pick up these Superior Crowns, place them upon our heads, and ask you to help us rule. We commission the angels to render these righteous verdicts in the spirit and the natural. We commission the angels to put this on record.

Thank you, Just Judge, for honoring us and trusting us with the responsibility of wearing these Crowns of Love and Righteousness. Thank you for helping us occupy the territory you assigned us. We don't take this lightly and ask for supernatural assistance and help daily to govern well as your sons, in the name of Jesus.

As a son, we call in the treasure that has been lost from the north, the south, the east, and the west in every age, realm, dimension, and time to fill the capacity of this section.

We ask that all of this be done in time and out of time, and in every age, realm, and dimension, and that all of the spiritual debris, residue, and essences that were left behind by this inferior crown and the spirits that came with it be destroyed utterly. We thank you, Father, for what you did, Jesus, for giving us authority and dominion here.

Characteristics of the Crown of Devouring

- This dragon uses a thrust.
- At the back of the crown were two gems that were mounted higher than the other gems on the crown—almost making them appear like horns. It gave this dragon the appearance of having horns.
- The head of this crown was seeking whom he may devour.

- He sniffs out the weak, sniffing out those on the edge, and seeking whom he can devour.
- He hunts after the sons.
- It's a fierce crown.
- This is a fierce crown in league with the sons of perdition—the ones that have given themselves over to darkness.
- He follows the stench of sin.
- If you have sin in your life, he can smell you.
- There are those *that follow darkness* and there are those *that fall into darkness*. There is a difference. This dragon hunts both.
- He has many crowns, and he seeks to devour.
- Most don't come back when they've had this crown put upon their head.
- It's lethal. That's what devouring does.
- With this crown, you lose all sensibility and sense of oneness.
- The most hardened of hearts wear this crown, this isn't just the atheistic view, this is <u>a hatred of God</u>, a turning away, and the true sons of perdition.
- It's not like the average sinner wears this crown.
- This dragon seeks to devour common sense commonalities in people's lives to be able to hear the voice of God, as well as see the voice of God.
- He devours truth.
- The darkest of the dark wear this crown.
- It's not the average atheist or sinner who wears this crown. This is like the deepest, darkest,

blackest-hearted people. The ones that consume babies and murder and are on a path of what we would call the evil ones.
- It works in tandem with all of the other crowns because it's the one that seeks to devour.
- There is no light in them. There is only darkness. You can sin, and it begins sniffing you out.
- The other crowns must be removed before this crown is addressed.
- Those who wear this crown have stepped over into something really dark purposefully.
- They have no conscience.

———— ∞ ————

Chapter 32

The False Crown of Magic (The Fifth Crown)

As we engaged Heaven for more revelation on false crowns, Stephanie saw a crown with purple stones mounted on it. The stones were the most beautiful color purple she had ever seen. The crown they were mounted on was beautiful, dark, and larger than the other crowns we had seen. It was apparent that this was important because from the back of the crown to the front, the stones were all the same size except for the one in the very front. The others were all mounted on different points, except the center stone. The middle point at the front of the crown was higher and had a beautiful, long, elongated purple stone, whereas all other stones were shorter. The crown itself was suspended in the air, and the scenery around it was black.

Even though its beauty enamored her, Stephanie realized this was not a good crown. She watched as it turned slowly in mid-air, as Heaven had her focus on all the points around the crown. It had flickers of light that were not light but flicks of a spark of some sort that were coming off of it. This was a *Crown of Magic*. It was the crown on the fifth head of the dragon.

John said, "Tantalizing, isn't it?"

She replied, "It was deceiving, for sure. Based on its intriguing nature, I was originally thinking it was a good crown."

"That's what makes this crown unique, the deception that comes with the witchcraft," he explained.

Stephanie noted, "Well, we've seen a Crown of Deception already."

"This crown is unique unto itself," John clarified. "The deception here is that many believe forms of witchcraft are good. We saw this culturally a few years ago with the popularity of the Harry Potter series. Years before, we were socially inoculated by the television show *Bewitched*. Growing up, we were taught the false narrative of a good witch versus a bad witch in the movie *The Wizard of Oz*. We have been pre-conditioned to the lie that there is good witchcraft and bad witchcraft. NO! It is all bad!

"The brides of Satan wear this crown. It has an allure to it. It lures them in. It's full of lust for power. It has an elevation to it. This crown suspends those who wear it. They are in a realm of darkness that looks like light to them. It feels like power. It entices their senses, and it is full of greed."

It is the most dishonoring of crowns as dishonor alights upon the heads of those that wear it, for they have indeed dishonored the Lord.

Stephanie asked John what the shimmers of light she saw sparking out were. He replied that with this crown, elements of truth pull them in.

When a lie is embedded in the truth, it makes it a lie.

The spirit of whoring is with this crown. It has an insatiable appetite and is handcrafted in hell.

Many of these crowns come through the assignments on the generational line where there has been a lot of witchcraft.

As Hosea wrote, "My people are destroyed for their lack of knowledge."[22]

He instructed us to have the sons remove these crowns from their generational line that came through bloodline iniquity and sin. Then, commission the angels to go and *blight* these crowns from the generational line. It is a blight in the bloodline where these crowns come from. Many lingering human spirits are attached to the generational line because of this crown.

When you remove the crowns through repentance, you remove the lingering human spirits who wear them. There's going to be a fight about it. They're not going to want to relinquish them. They have been empowered by these crowns operating on and through the generational line. However, they will be removed.

Know that blight is something that destroys or impairs. When that crown is on the bloodline, it seeks to destroy. Remember, light dispels the darkness.

This crown also has a throne that needs to be dismantled. It is very much like an altar.

---

[22] Hosea 4:6

Prayer for Removal of the Crown of Magic

Father, we ask to step into your Court of Mercy, through Jesus, on behalf of the generations. We ask that the accuser of the brethren be brought in as well as our generational line, from both sides of the family, and those who are with us by blood, marriage, adoption, civil or religious covenant, from your hand in the garden and to your hand in the future. Your Honor, we agree with the adversary that we were deceived by magic and everything it encompasses.

We repent for magic, for the use of it, for the places in the generations that yielded to it, utilized it, for those who took it up, that felt empowered by it, that were deceived because of it, and for those that elevated themselves in believing the lie.

We repent for those in the generations who practiced magic but also deceived others with bits of truth to pull them into the lie. We repent on their behalf.

We repent on behalf of everyone who believed the lie, succumbed to it, and then projected it, and perpetuated it through the generational line.

We repent for agreeing with the spirit of whoring, for trading with it, for seducing because of it, and for allowing it.

We repent for the garments they wore. We ask that they be removed and destroyed now.

We repent, sir, all the way back to Your hand and all the way forward. Lord, we repent for taking this inferior crown and for the use of this crown. Where they saw it as useful, yet it was a lie.

We repent where we put this inferior crown on other people's heads and our own.

On behalf of the lingering human spirits who are or who are not a part of our bloodline, as well as our generations who are now assigned to the bloodline because of taking up these inferior crowns. We repent on their behalf for every sin under the sun, which is egregious in nature, which dishonored and brought dishonor to the Lord because of taking up and for wearing these inferior crowns.

We commission the angels to go through the timelines, ages, and dimensions for every person who wore this inferior crown, and we commission you to take it off their heads as we stand before the Lord in repentance for them. We forgive, bless, and release them.

We ask the angels to open up the silver channel, take the demonic guard and the bosses who were assigned to these LHS's, to Jesus' feet for judgment. To every lingering human spirit in the generational line, you will go and see Jesus today. You are not staying.

We forgive you, bless you, and release you for what you were doing in and through the bloodline. You are removed this day by the hand of God because of repentance, which we are allowed to do. He forgave us, and we forgive you.

When you see Jesus, we suggest you ask Him for mercy. Angels, we commission you to destroy every inferior Crown of Witchcraft in the name of Jesus.

We ask for a Crown of Truth to be given to our generational line—the utter and distinct truth, the Superior Crown that causes all other inferior crowns to be dismantled and destroyed, as their knee must bow, in the name of Jesus.

We ask that the thrones and mantles be found, dismantled, and destroyed in every place throughout the generational line.

Where our generations set this up as a type of altar, we ask that it be destroyed, and that every attendant of every altar be captured and dealt with according to the will of the Father, and that the idol of witchcraft, as well as this Crown of Magic, be judged in the courts today.

We commission the angels to take every spirit or entity who has been assigned or associated with this throne, inferior crown, mantle, and scepter to be taken to court for judgment. We commission the angels to destroy the thrones forever, and that the altar of the Lord be established in their place, in and through the bloodline. We request that angels be assigned there to worship and that the Crown of Truth be established as it sits upon the altar of the Lord.

We request that every false scepter that came with this inferior crown and this throne, which was considered to be a wand, also be taken from the generational bloodline and be utterly destroyed, annulled, and removed. We ask that its frequency be dismantled and destroyed in the name of Jesus.

We request the realm of the inferior hovering crown, the realm from which it came, be closed and that there be a closed, sealed door in and upon the line of the generations forevermore with no ability to reopen.

We request that the center stone of this inferior crown, which is the eye, be utterly crushed, annulled, canceled, destroyed, and blinded forever in, though, and upon the generational line.

We ask for the amendment of 'As if it Never Were.'

We ask for our righteous verdicts or further counsel.

[If further counsel is advised, follow these instructions. Once you have received a righteous verdict, begin the following segment:]

We speak to the earth, water, air, and fire. We have received a righteous verdict, and since the world and the fullness of it belong to the Lord, we charge you to swallow up, drown, blow away and burn all evil words, deeds, lies, witchcraft, innocent bloodshed, sexual sins, occultic cauldrons, evil rooms, evil technologies, spells, hexes, vexes, incantations, voodoo, dark art, manipulation, monitoring, astral projections, evil projections, counterfeit intelligence, and any and all other darkness or evil done upon the Earth, through the air, to the water and using fire.

We bless you to the fullness of your original design and charge you to bless us as the Lord walks through time, restoring it and you to their fullness. We do this in the name and blood of Jesus and as governing sons.

As a son, we call in the treasure that has been lost from the north, the south, the east, and the west in every age, realm, dimension, and time to fill the capacity of this section.

We ask that all of this be done in time and out of time, and in every age, realm, and dimension, and that all of the spiritual debris, residue, and essences left behind by this inferior crown and the spirits that came with it be destroyed utterly. We thank you, Father, for what you did, Jesus, for giving us authority and dominion here.

Stephanie then saw that the angel took the center stone out of its mounting and crushed it. That's why there is a throne associated with this crown; it is a seat of its power.

The thing about the enemy is that *he doesn't trust anyone*, so embedded in this crown was the eye for him to see what they do for him. It's like a back-and-forth messaging. Because he doesn't trust anyone, he sets up a monitoring system in each crown. It is a wicked technology.

Characteristics of the False Crown of Magic

- It has purple stones mounted on it.
- The stones are a beautiful color purple.
- The crown is beautiful, dark, and larger than the other crowns.
- The very middle point at the front of the crown was higher and had a beautiful long, elongated purple stone, whereas all of the other stones were shorter.
- This is not a good crown.
- It is a tantalizing, seducing crown.
- That's what makes this crown unique, the deception that comes with the witchcraft.
- This crown is unique unto itself.
- The deception here is that many believe forms of witchcraft are good.
- The brides of Satan wear this crown.
- It has an allure to it. It lures them in.
- It's full of lust for power.
- It has an elevation to it.
- This crown suspends those that wear it.
- They are in a realm of darkness that looks like light to them.
- It feels like power.
- It entices their senses.
- It is full of greed.
- It is the most dishonoring of crowns as dishonor alights upon the heads of those that wear it, for they have indeed dishonored the Lord.

- This crown contains elements of truth that pull people in. However, when a lie is embedded in the truth, it makes the entire thing a lie.
- The spirit of whoring is with this crown.
- It has an insatiable appetite and is handcrafted in hell.
- Many of these crowns come through the assignments on the generational line where there has been a lot of witchcraft.
- Many lingering human spirits are on the generational line because of this crown.
- This crown's center stone is a seat and an eye of its power.
- It is a blight that destroys and impairs.
- This crown also has a throne that needs to be dismantled. It is very much like an altar.
- There is a throne associated with this crown; it is a seat of its power.
- It is embedded in distrust.
- He uses the main stone as a monitoring system.
- It is a wicked technology.

———— ∞ ————

Chapter 33

The False Crown of Secrets

(The Sixth Crown)

As we began our engagement in the Library of Revelation, John informed us, "There is an inferior crown unlike any other. It is quiet and stealthy. It silences the sons. It seeks to silence. It is bloodthirsty, and it screams of desire to pierce the frequencies. It walks with the spirit of death. Its inner workings are harlotry, divination, and mockery."

Stephanie asked, "Are you showing me where excoriation fits in here? It's not a word I use."

"The sounds of intercession rub and excoriate this head of this dragon, which was why it seeks to silence the sons," John explained. "The Pharisees wore this crown with their lofty robes. Violence comes from the mouth of this dragon who wears this crown."

We asked, "John, will you tell us the name of this crown?"

Stephanie remarked, "I've still been sitting here at the table with my head down. It is very unlike the other engagements where I was facing and seeing this dragon. But my chair is now turned, and I see the sixth head and the fourth head (the Crown of Antichrist). These two work together. John, which head of the dragon is this one? I see that they work together."

The Crown of Secrets works in tandem with the Crown of Antichrist.

He replied, "This is the sixth. This dragon's head has a cloak around it to make it hidden."

This is the seat of Freemasonry, so it has a throne. It is shrouded in secrecy.

We have found that various degree levels of Freemasonry have crowns.

Stephanie noted that the head of this dragon had an eerie smirk to it.

John continued, "It revels in its deception. It's the Crown of Secrets. What do secrets do in correlation to silencing?"

"Well, when you have a secret, you're quiet about it," Stephanie answered. "I see this dragon throw its head back, and in this crown is fantasy that cooperates with harlotry. This is the defilement of the imagination. This crown not only seeks silence but also mocks the sons. Its mouth is full of corruption, indignity, and falsehood. It's stealthy in nature."

John insisted, "Tell the readers that every secret will be brought to light. Secrets shroud, but the uncovering is unbearable. It is the Lord who uncovers that many times."

It is this head of the dragon that seeks to shame and silence the sons. Have no secrets within you.

Recently, the pastor of a large church in the Dallas/Fort Worth area was forced to resign due to something that happened with an underaged woman many years ago. His secret came out and silenced and shamed him.

The old saying, "Be sure your sin will find you out" has much truth in it.

Remove and utterly destroy this crown from your heads. It is unbecoming of a son.

James 5:16:

> **Confess your trespasses to one another**, and pray for one another, that you may be healed. The effective, fervent prayer of a righteous man avails much. (Emphasis mine)

John walked around where Stephanie saw the dragon and picked the crown up off this dragon's head. He paused and she could see him reflecting in his heart about something. He said, "Crush this serpent under your feet," and he put the crown on the ground, and he stepped on it. She could hear it crackling under his feet.

The sons bear the responsibility of secrets.

Deuteronomy 29:29:

> *The secret things belong to the LORD our God, but those things which are revealed belong to us and to our children forever, that we may do all the words of this law.*

Psalms 25:14:

> *The secret of the LORD is with those who fear Him, and He will show them His covenant.*

Don't fall into its trap. *Govern* this crown, remove it, destroy it.

John began to walk away. Stephanie noted that there was a real seriousness here, a reverential fear. She looked at what was left of this crown on the ground, and she realized regret was in that crown.

Prayer for Removal of the Crown of Secrets

Father, we ask for access to your Court of Mercy today. I want to repent on behalf of me and my generations, who kept secrets and took this crown willingly. We reveled in harlotry, took on shame, co-labored with deception, allowed it to mock, and caused our own silencing of Your voice. As governing sons, forgive us and our generations for the secrets and for even having secrets about other people and using those secrets against them.

We repent for not taking this crown off our own heads, not confessing our sins one to another so that we could be healed, not confessing these things to you. We harbored them in our hearts and acted like you didn't know. We repent where we acted like you couldn't see, and where we kept a secret, and we even smiled about it and reveled in it.

Forgive us and our generations and forgive us where we took the throne and the seat of Freemasonry within our generations and did not present the throne and the crown to you.

We take it, and we crush it—this inferior crown under our feet—the head of the snake, the head of this dragon, we crush it and present to you the throne and request that the angels utterly destroy it and the altar and the idols of secrecy be judged in Your court this day as we repent on behalf of the generations for they did not really know what they were doing. We ask that a complete capture of every demonic spirit that was used be made. Forgive us where your voice through us was silenced.

Because of this, we ask that angels crush shame and regret, and we ask for the amendment of 'As if it Never Were' as your blood pours through our generations, that the angels would go and remove every single Crown of Secrets in the bloodline and destroy it.

Forgive us when we uncovered other people and brought them shame because of the secret we knew about. We accept Father the scripture that everything that is done in secret is brought to light—your light. We ask this in the name of Jesus.

We thank you, Father, we thank you, Jesus, and we thank you, John, for your transparency as we are learning that transparency is godly—no secrets.

We repent for any and all cooperation with Baal in any form at any time. We turn our back to the altar of Baal and ask angels to destroy every altar of Baal. We ask for a divorce from Baal, Lucifer, the red dragon, the Book of Magic, and any ungodly attraction. We ask that all debris associated with this cooperation with Baal be removed and destroyed on our behalf. We remove the regalia *associated with this ungodly marriage covenant and request to be clothed in robes of righteousness.*

We request that the head of this snake be cut off from the other heads and from this dragon.

We ask for your righteous verdict or further counsel.

[If further counsel is advised, follow these instructions. Once you have received a righteous verdict, begin the following segment:]

We speak to the Earth that every one of our generations stepped upon, even those related to us by blood, marriage, adoption, civil or religious covenant.

Earth, we have received a righteous verdict from the Courts of Heaven this day. We bless you to hear the word of the Lord. We bless you to swallow up the iniquity and the egregious sins of self-deception and wearing these inferior crowns. Swallow up every word and deed that was done upon you. Swallow the innocent bloodshed, sexual sins, moving of the boundary stones, worship of ourselves, idol worship, occultic worship, theft—every sin under the sun that Jesus died for. We charge you to swallow it up and bless you to your original design. We bless you to see the governing sons and to begin blessing us. Begin pouring out your riches of abundance of truth and life.

We request the blood of Jesus to cover every place this was done upon you or in you. We speak to the frequencies of the wind to blow away the evil, to the water to drown it, and to the fire to burn it. We speak to you to return to your original design as the Lord had created you. The Earth is the Lord's, and its fullness belongs to the Lord.

We speak peace. We thank the Just Judge. We thank you, Jesus, the author and the finisher of our faith, for the Crowns of Righteousness and the Crown of Love that trump this inferior crown.

As governing sons, we pick up these Superior Crowns, place them upon our heads, and ask you to help us rule. We commission the angels to render these righteous verdicts in the spirit and the natural. We commission the angels to put this on record.

Thank you, Just Judge, for honoring us and trusting us with the responsibility of wearing these Crowns of Love and Righteousness. Thank you for helping us occupy the territory you assigned us. We don't take this lightly and ask for supernatural assistance and help daily to govern well as your sons, in the name of Jesus.

As a son, we call in the treasure that has been lost from the north, the south, the east, and the west in every age, realm, dimension, and time to fill the capacity of this section.

We ask that all of this be done in time and out of time, and in every age, realm, and dimension, and that all of the spiritual debris, residue, and essences that were left behind by this inferior crown and the spirits that came with it be destroyed utterly. We thank you, Father, for what you did, Jesus, for giving us authority and dominion here.

John made Stephanie look at him, and he said, "These secrets are nothing but lies. There's no truth in them. If this head has a secret, he is not revealing it."

However, Mark 4:22 says:

> *For there **is nothing that is hidden that won't be disclosed,** and **there is no secret that won't be brought out into the light!** (Emphasis mine)*

We knew we had one more crown to learn about, but a summary of the characteristics of this crown is in order.

Instructions to the Sons:

- Remove and utterly destroy this crown from your heads. It is unbecoming of a son.
- Repent for any involvement with this crown at any time, in any fashion, in any place.
- You are to govern this crown, then remove it, then destroy it.
- Crush this serpent under your feet.

Characteristics of the Crown of Secrets

- It seeks to silence the sons.

- It mocks the sons.
- It seeks to shame the sons
- It is bloodthirsty.
- Its screams of desire pierce frequencies.
- It walks with the spirit of death.
- Its inner workings are harlotry, divination, and mockery.
- Intercession of the sons excoriates the head of the dragon.
- Pharisees wore this crown.
- Violence comes from the mouth of this dragon to those who wear this crown.
- It covers itself with a cloak.
- It is the seat of Freemasonry that has a throne.
- It is shrouded.
- It revels in its deception.
- It is involved in the defilement of the imagination.
- Its mouth is full of corruption, indignity, and falsehood.
- It is stealthy in nature.
- Its secrets are nothing but lies.
- There is no truth in it.
- Regret is in this crown.
- It is the primary crown of Freemasonry.

———— ∞ ————

Chapter 34

The False Crown of Antichrist (The Fourth Crown)

Stephanie began, "Thank you, Father, as we ask to step into the realms of Heaven through you, Jesus. We ask to step into the Library of Revelation to find out what Heaven has to say about crowns, territories, dominion, mantles, thrones, and the revelation regarding the last head of the dragon. I call all of our angels near. I invite The Seven Spirits of God to help me.

"Are you here, John?"

John replied, "Intrigued, are we?"

Stephanie responded, "Yes, we are. We're intrigued."

He added, "It is right for Dr. Ron not to want to give the enemy (the red dragon being on the front of the new Crown book) credit because, after all, it's just a principality." (He said this in response to a recommendation that I have a picture of a red dragon on the cover of this book, but I declined, saying, "I don't want to give him the press.")

Stephanie responded, "Wow. It's true."

"Do you want to sit or stand for this encounter?" John inquired.

"What does Heaven want me to do?" She asked in return. (Heaven is constantly teaching us to ask questions and make statements like this. Heaven will still give us free will.) "Okay, so I'm going to sit down." As she sat, she noticed her chair was turning toward the bookcase, which was opening.

Through the opening, she could see the fourth head of the dragon highlighted. She could also see *all* the heads, but this head was highlighted and its neck and head were gold in color.

Stephanie asked, "Why would it be gold? The long, elongated neck and the head are gold."

"This crown is full of pomp and circumstance," John answered. "There's an *elitism* to those who wear this crown. They have a 'Better than you' attitude."

Stephanie described, "The way Heaven is showing the head of this dragon to me is that the dragon is looking down at people."

He responded, "It has an air of superiority and a superiority complex." (Not unlike the Sadducees and teachers of the Law in the New Testament.)

"John, is this different than the selves in the False Crown of Deceit?"

John replied, "Much different. This is the crown that the antichrist will wear.

"Indoctrinated, indoctrinated, indoctrinated. Those who wear this crown *are indoctrinated*. The ones with this crown have multiple purposes. It works with the Crown of Secrets on the sixth head, and it also works with the Crown of Deceit found on the first head. The ones who wear this Crown can easily put on the Crown of Deception. This crown is noteworthy."

Stephanie inserted, "I know that has multiple meanings."

"This crown clings to the cross but in defilement," he continued. "It is superstitious, seeks fame, is pretentious, full of pride, lofty, arrogant, and judges. This crown *has the deadliest bite,* and this crown *has infiltrated the church*. This crown calls in the Delilah's, the Jezebel's, and the Ahab's."

Stephanie asked, "John, can you tell me the name of this crown?"

"It has the deadliest bite. In its bite, there are many poisons. This crown *has led more astray* than any of the other crowns."

She interjected, "That's what makes it noteworthy. I keep hearing the word antichrist. Is this the Crown of Antichrist?"

"It is."

"So, this is a Crown of Antichrist. I like the fact that it's not the Crown of Religion. It's not something I made up."

John answered, "It embodies false religion.

This crown has the deadliest bite.

"It has a realm.

---
*It is the **Crown** of Antichrist,
there is a **Realm** of Antichrist
and a **Spirit** of Antichrist
as well as an **Office** of Antichrist.*

"Many would believe that the unsaved wear this crown, but it is upon those embodied in the church, upon those with the deadly bite, and those that co-conspire with the spirit, the office, and the realm of the antichrist.

"It has polluted the church, the Body of Christ, and the Ecclesia. Those who are bitten by those who wear this crown often leave the Body of Christ and never return. In the last several years, you have probably heard or known of pastors who suddenly announced they no longer believe in God. They have taken this crown.

---

*Its main goal and focus
are to bring an end
to the embodiment of the body,
which is the church.*

---

*Remove not only its mantle,
the crown, and its seat,
which is a throne,
but also the Delilah's.*

"Focus on the repentance work and on the work of those in the body of Christ who have been elevated to positions and seats of power. Also to those who have ruling and rank over the people, and to those who have tolerated Jezebel.[23] But also *close the portal, remove its garments,* and *request that the head of this snake be cut off from the rest.* It empowers and it emboldens those

---

[23] See Revelation 2:20 – toleration of Jezebel implies toleration of sexual sin in essentially any form, self-gratification, pornography, fornication, adultery, incest, homosexuality, bestiality, etc.

whose lust *is* power and greed, and it enslaves those under it," John instructed.

---

*You must break off
the chains of enslavement
from this crown for the people.*

Stephanie remarked, "If I could just show you the picture that they put in my mind about what this thing is and what it looks like because this dragon's head is upright, it is flanked in gold, and it has this personification of being better than the other heads, and it's more beautiful, lofty and crafty. It seems like it wouldn't be fearsome feeling when encountering it. It's not, but John keeps saying that its bite is deadly and poisonous."

I asked, "Are there particular ways it works with the Crown of Secrets?"

Stephanie replied, "He immediately showed me Freemasonry in the church. I saw various spiritual leaders, pastors, and clergy who are Freemasons. This crown will reach over and literally put onto people's heads the Crown of Deceit or Deception.

"He showed me that the fourth crown works specifically with the sixth crown (the Crown of Secrets) and the first crown (the Crown of Deceit or Deception) on the heads of this dragon. You must be delusional, have delusions of grandeur, and be secretive. How many pastors and how many churches have been covered in secrets?"

John continued, "It's not just about removing this crown; you must *remove its mantle, destroy the seat,* and *close the portal.* You must *break the chains from those who have been impacted or who have been in agreement with one who wears this crown* and *those who were over you.*"

Steps to Freedom from the Fourth Crown.

In order to remove this crown, you must:

1. Remove its mantle.
2. Destroy the seat.
3. Close the portal.
4. Break the chains.

Stephanie queried, "It all must be done through repentance work. Wouldn't you think that this is key for when we are doing work for a city? This crown has an office, too—the Crown of Antichrist. Thank you, John.

"I feel much better," she continued. "I felt the pressure of gaining an understanding of this crown. That's why all the crowns must be on a person's head for the destroyer crown to work; you would have to have the Crown of Antichrist, too. But John, the people that I saw with the destroyer crown were people that are like the Luciferians, the people that are the worst of the worst. They're not going to church or are over churches."

John asked, "Where in this engagement did we say that it was just clergy?"

Stephanie replied, "You didn't. There are some clergy members in it. You were saying everything that comes with this crown and who might wear it. Thank you, John."

"Wait until we show you the woman in the Book of Revelation."

"John is laughing," she described. "You're kidding, right?"

I responded, "No, he is not."

With that, the bookcase closed, and Stephanie heard the sound of a locking mechanism.

Prayer for Removal of the Crown of Antichrist

Father, we ask to step into the Mercy Court of Heaven to receive Mercy in our time of need. We request the accuser of the brethren be brought in as well as our entire generations and everyone related to us by blood, marriage, adoption, civil or religious covenant, all the way back to Your hand in the garden, and all the way forward to Your hand.

Your Honor, we agree with the adversary that we and our generations bowed our knees to this dragon, accepted the inferior crowns, and wore them proudly. We repent for the spirit of antichrist we bore and the inferior crown we took upon our heads. We repent for the pomp and circumstance, elitism, better than you attitude, superior and superiority complex, indoctrination we took on, as well as the indoctrination of others; we repent for embodying a false religion and for 'biting' those we were in stewardship over, releasing the poison. We repent for working with the false Crown of Delusion as well as the false Crown of Secrets. We repent for all of the secrets this inferior crown bore that we agreed with.

We repent for conspiring with the office, realm and spirit of antichrist, for embodying it. We repent for participating in exploiting, polluting, and poisoning the church, the body, and the ecclesia. We repent for being a part of an end to bodies of ecclesias, people, and churches. We repent for allowing, tolerating, being in league, and cooperating with the Delilah, Jezebel, and Ahab spirits. We repent for opening up an evil portal and for creating evil timelines for us, our generations, and for others. We repent for taking on this mantle, sitting on the seat/office/throne and ruling unjustly over your people. We repent for seeking to be elevated to positions and seats of power or where we, who wore this inferior crown, elevated those who should not ever have been elevated. We repent for the pride, and for lusting power and greed.

We repent for the false clinging to the cross, the defilement and mockery of it, for seeking fame, being pretentious, full of pride, lofty, arrogant, and judging others. We repent for embodying false religion, for promoting and esteeming it. Forgive us and our generations for infiltrating the church, bringing this inferior crown and elevating others to it. Forgive us for leading others astray.

We request your blood, Jesus, the amendment of 'As If It Never Were,' the destruction of the seat/office/throne, the closing of the portal, and the removal of the garments. Please remove its mantle, destroy the seat, and close the portal. We ask that you break the chains from those who have been impacted or who have agreed with those who have worn this inferior crown over the generations and those whom we were over.

Please have these destroyed. We request that the chains attached to us and our generations be cut, severed, destroyed, dismantled, and the ashes of them be brought to Jesus. We request a full destruction, annulment, cancellation and overturning of the office of the Crown of Antichrist, in the name of Jesus.

We also request that the angels clean up the spiritual debris, essences, and residues in time, out of time and in every age, realm, and dimension to infinity. Burn it and give the ashes to Jesus.

We ask for your righteous verdict or further counsel.

[If further repentance is needed, follow instructions of the court.]

With our righteous verdict in hand, we speak to the Earth. We speak to you that every one of our generations who stepped upon you, even those related to us by blood, marriage, adoption, civil or religious covenant. Earth, we have received a righteous verdict from the Courts of Heaven this day.

We bless you to hear the word of the Lord. We bless you to swallow up the iniquity and the egregious sins of wearing these inferior crowns. Swallow up every word and deed that was done upon you. Swallow the innocent bloodshed, sexual sins, moving of the boundary stones, worship of ourselves, idol worship, occultic worship, theft—every sin under the sun that Jesus died for.

We charge you to swallow it up, and we bless you to your original design; we bless you to see the governing sons and to begin blessing us. Begin pouring out your riches of the abundance of the truth of life. We request the blood of Jesus to cover every place this was done upon you, in you. We speak to the frequencies of the wind to blow away the evil. To the water, to drown it, and to the fire to burn it. We speak to you to come back to your original design as the Lord had created you, the Earth. The Earth is the Lord's and the fullness of it belong to the Lord.

We speak peace and we thank you, Jesus. We thank the Just Judge. We thank you, Jesus, the author and the finisher of our faith. We commission the angels to render these righteous verdicts in the spirit and the natural.

We commission the angels to put this on record. Thank you, Just Judge, for honoring us and trusting us with the responsibility of wearing the Crown of Love and Crown of Righteousness. Thank you for helping us occupy the territory you assigned us. We don't take this lightly and ask for supernatural assistance and help daily to govern well as your sons, in the name of Jesus.

As a son, we call in the treasure that has been lost from the north, the south, the east, and the west in every age, realm, dimension, and time to fill the capacity of this section.

We are grateful to Heaven for revealing the red dragon, its inferior crowns, and its mission. We are grateful that Revelation tells us that this dragon has been pierced by God himself. Thank you for your kindness in helping us overcome the word of our testimony and the blood of the lamb.

We ask that all of this be done in time and out of time, and in every age, realm, and dimension, and that all of the spiritual debris, residue, and essences that were left behind by this inferior crown and the spirits that came with it be destroyed utterly. We thank you, Father, for what you did, Jesus, for giving us authority and dominion here.

When I prayed this, I heard an unlocking. I saw myself being unlocked from this dragon, from the chains on me and my generations. I had a knowing that the locking I heard earlier when the bookcase closed, was the understanding of the end of this particular engagement, and this unlocking I just heard was an unlocking to the dragon. The dragon and its seven heads can be fully locked away from us with the amendment of 'As If It Never Were'! Praise Jesus!

Characteristics of the False Crown of Antichrist

- This crown is full of pomp and circumstance.
- There's an elitism to those who wear this crown, a 'Better than you' attitude.'
- It has an air of superiority and a superiority complex.
- This is the crown that the antichrist will wear.
- Those that wear this crown are indoctrinated.
- The ones with this crown have multiple purposes.
- It works with the crown on the sixth head (Crown of Secrets), and it also works with the crown on the first head (Crown of Deception).
- The ones that wear this crown are easily able to put on the Crown of Deception from the first head.
- This crown is noteworthy.
- This crown clings to the cross but in defilement.
- It is superstitious.
- It seeks fame.
- It is pretentious. It is full of pride.

- It is lofty.
- It is arrogant.
- It judges.
- This crown has the deadliest bite.
- In its bite, there are many poisons.
- This crown has infiltrated the church.
- This crown calls in the Delilah's, the Jezebel's, and the Ahab's.
- This crown has led more astray than any of the other crowns.
- It embodies false religion.
- It has a realm.
- It empowers.
- It emboldens those whose lust is power and greed.
- It enslaves those under it.
- There is a Crown of antichrist, realm of antichrist, spirit of antichrist, and office of antichrist.
- It is embodied upon those in the church.
- It has polluted the church, the Body of Christ, and the Ecclesia.
- Those that are bitten by those who wear this crown often leave the Body of Christ and never return.
- Its main goal and focus are to bring an end to the embodiment of the body, which is the church.

Solutions

- Remove not only its mantle, the crown, and its seat, which is a throne, but also the Delilah's.
- Focus on the repentance work of those in the body of Christ who have been elevated to positions and seats of power, to those who have ruling and rank over the people, and to those who have tolerated Jezebel.
- Close the portal.
- Remove its garments.
- Request that the head of this snake be cut off from the rest.

You must break off the chains of enslavement from this crown for the people.

———— ∞ ————

Chapter 35
Prayer of Freedom from the Seven False Crowns

If you have prayed the prayers of freedom from all seven of the false crowns, you may want to wrap up the prayer work in this manner:

Father, we ask to step into Your Court of Crowns. We ask that the accuser of the brethren be brought into this court as well as our generations, those related to us by blood, marriage, civil and religious covenant, all the way back to Your hand in the garden and all the way forward to Your hand.

We ask that the seven-headed dragon be brought in and muzzled and caged. We request that the accuser of the brethren and every Principality, power, demon, ruler of darkness, and evil entity that was associated with the seven-headed dragon, their inferior crowns, mantles, altars, thrones, and scepters, be brought in and gagged as well.

Having done repentance work for each of the seven crowns, Your Honor, we are asking that the repentance work already accomplished, and the verdicts be brought into evidence in this court this day. We also request our cloud of witnesses, the angels and every witness to these events be brought into this court on our behalf.

We request that these seven heads be judged today, for they have inflicted pain, torment, anguish, and untold misery upon your sons and daughters and the peoples of the Earth. They have hindered the growth, abilities, expansion, and work of your church on Earth. They have murdered, stolen, and destroyed without regard for You, Your sons, or Your purposes in the Earth. They have laid evil and egregious crowns on the heads of your sons to mock not only them but You.

We ask that each head be judged, cut off, and destroyed from our lives, and the damage be undone via the amendment of 'As if it Never Were.'

We ask that you please burn the inferior Crown of the Beast which is set above the seven-headed dragon, the dragon, its seven heads, its inferior crowns, thrones, mantles, scepters, altars, spiritual residue, essences, and debris. In Jesus' name, we ask for the Superior Crowns of the Kingdom of Heaven to be placed on our heads, overturning the egregiousness of our sins.

We ask for renewed authorization for every crown restored to us and those to be restored today in your court.

We are grateful to Heaven for revealing the red dragon, its inferior crowns, associated evil entities, and its mission. We are grateful that Revelation tells us that this dragon has been pierced by God Himself. Thank you for your kindness in helping us overcome by the word of our testimony and the blood of the lamb.

We ask that all of this be done in time and out of time, and in every age, realm, and dimension, and that all the spiritual debris, residue, and essences that were left behind by this inferior crown and the spirits that came with it be destroyed utterly. We also ask that these evil entities be judged in your court this day, in Jesus' name.

We thank you, Father, for what you did, Jesus, for giving us the authority and dominion here.

———— ∞ ————

Chapter 36

Crown of Righteousness

We had finished learning about the seven crowns on the head of the red dragon and wanted to know about any other crowns. Immediately, Stephanie heard the question, "What do you know about the Crown of Righteousness?"

She replied, "Well, I know we are only righteous because of you, Jesus."

"Would you say that the Crown of Faith plays a role in this?"

"I'm sure it does," she replied. "Will you explain it to us?"

Heaven said, "What if we were to tell you that wearing the Crown of Righteousness causes a bird's eye view within the Father's heart of only seeing Jesus? He only sees Jesus when looking at you. How you see yourselves is not part of the equation." Isn't it good to know that His righteousness causes us to look like Jesus? That is good news!

Picture this: Even in your darkest times, the Father sees you as Jesus. He is in you. You are in Him, and together, you are in the Father. Picture this bird's eye view. How, then, could you say that the Father is against you? Or that He can never forgive you, when He only sees Jesus? The crown on your head is His display of Jesus. Seeking His righteousness places this crown upon your head.

Matthew 6:33:

> *So above all, constantly chase after the realm of God's kingdom and the righteousness that proceeds from him. Then all these less important things will be given to you abundantly. (TPT)*

Now, here is a plot twist. You must also picture this Crown of Righteousness upon the heads of those who love Jesus, even those who hurt you. The same picture He *views you* through this crown, He *views them as well*. As you do this, it is a form of seeking righteousness, seeking it upon the heads of others, viewing it, seeing it, embracing it. The more you do this, the more love will abound in all relationships.

---

*In no way does failure
remove this crown from you.*

It is set upon the heads of the sons *forevermore* because it is not in and of yourselves that allotted this crown to you, *but that of Jesus Christ*. So, see yourself with this forever crown upon the heads of others, and love will abound.

Our teacher in this segment was not identified to us, so I had Stephanie ask them about the Crown of Faith that had been mentioned earlier. Gloria, our legal counsel, replied, "The Crown of Faith is no small thing, but yet it is." Stephanie described what appeared to be a minuscule crown the size of a mustard seed.

She continued, "When you present the crown, even as a mustard seed, watch it grow."

As Stephanie watched, it began to grow. We can view the Crown of Faith as a mustard seed that grows as she had seen. As we step into this walk of faith, the Crown of Faith is given to us. There is a grace around this Crown of Faith. Faith will abound. The Crown of Faith works with the Crown of Righteousness.

Matthew 13:31-32:

> [31] *Another parable He put forth to them, saying: 'The kingdom of heaven is like a mustard seed, which a man took and sowed in his field,* [32] *which indeed is the least of all the seeds; but when it is grown it is greater than the herbs and becomes a tree so that the birds of the air come and nest in its branches.' (TPT)*

Matthew 17:20:

So Jesus said to them, 'Because of your unbelief; for assuredly, I say to you, if you have faith as a mustard seed, you will say to this mountain, 'Move from here to there,' and it will move; and nothing will be impossible for you.' (TPT)

Romans 1:17:

For in it, the righteousness of God is revealed from faith to faith; as it is written, 'THE JUST SHALL LIVE BY FAITH.' (TPT)

Take the measure of faith and see it as a quantity, like a measure of grain. When we take the little crown as a mustard seed and present it to God, it grows and grows, and the crown is then placed on our head. He takes what we give Him, and it begins to grow.

Now, take a situation where you need to exercise your faith and envision this little Crown of Faith. Release your faith in His faith and watch it begin to grow. Where you did not have the capacity to believe at first, now the capacity is enlarging, and the Crown of Faith is becoming large enough to fit on your head. Remember, your Crown of Righteousness is at work on your behalf, so the Father sees Jesus when looking at you. You have what you say.

Mark 11:22-26:

[22] Jesus replied, 'Let the faith of God be in you!

²³ Listen to the truth I speak to you: If someone says to this mountain with great faith and having no doubt, 'Mountain, be lifted up and thrown into the midst of the sea,' and believes that what he says will happen, it will be done.

²⁴ This is the reason I urge you to boldly believe for whatever you ask for in prayer—believe that you have received it, and it will be yours. ²⁵ And whenever you stand praying, if you find that you carry something in your heart against another person, release him and forgive him so that your Father in Heaven will also release you and forgive you of your faults.

²⁶ But if you will not release forgiveness, don't expect your Father in Heaven to release you from your misdeeds.'

According to verse 22, it is God's faith anyway! The only thing that can interfere is unforgiveness toward someone. Clear that up and watch the Crown of Faith grow in your life.

---

*The Crown of Faith works
with the Crown of Righteousness.*

The Crown of Faith works with the Crown of Righteousness in that as we embrace the fact that when the Father sees us, He sees Jesus and all He did for us through the cross and the resurrection. Our faith in that accomplished work grows, and the Crown of Faith becomes a constant adornment upon our heads in the spirit realm. It is an exercise of faith in the work of righteousness completed on our behalf. We were co-crucified, we co-died, we were co-raised, and now are co-seated at the Father's right hand. That's your new place of residence—enjoy your new home.

———— ∞ ————

Chapter 37
Retrieving Lost Crowns

In the first couple of chapters, we went straight to the issue of recovering lost, stolen, or forfeited crowns. This chapter repeats those steps for your use.

We have learned that crowns represent dominions, and with a crown comes authorization to exercise Kingdom authority within that dominion. Do all crowns have mantles and thrones?

An additional issue we will deal with is when Satan has captured one of our crowns and then once he is done parading around in it, he may place it in a trophy case in hell so that he can gloat over his victory regarding that crown.

Often, the enemy will place items such as crowns in trophy cases to ridicule the original owner of the crown. To successfully retrieve these captured trophies, we must repent for our mistakes that allowed their capture. Then, we must request angels to go and retrieve the crown from the trophy case and bring it to the Court of Crowns, where it can be cleansed of all defilements and returned to us along with the renewed or restored authorization of the crown and the authority it carries.

Retrieval from a Trophy Case

1. **Repent** for our mistakes that allowed its capture, then
2. **Request** angels to go and retrieve the crown from the trophy case.
3. **Request access** to the Court of Crowns:
   a. **Request it be cleansed** of all defilements and
   b. Be **returned** to us
4. **Request** the renewed or restored authorization of the crown along with the authority it carries.

Retrieving Lost Crowns

1. **Repent** for any part we held in losing our crown(s).
2. **Gain access to the Court of Crowns** and
3. **Request renewed authorization** for the authority that had been lost.
4. **Commission the angels** to bring in what has been lost and fill the capacity. That capacity can also be enlarged.

I am convinced that we have much more to learn about crowns, but as we exercise what we know, more understanding will come. Let us step into the Court of Crowns, repossess the crowns Heaven has in mind for us, and receive the reauthorization of any lost or forfeited crowns. Then, step into the crown's authority and further establish the Kingdom of God upon the Earth.

May you retrieve every lost, stolen, or forfeited crown and step into new levels of sonship beginning today!

———— ∞ ————

Appendix

Learning to Live Spirit First

Achallenge with how we were taught about the Christian life is that everything was put off until sometime in the future. Then, we read the letters of Paul, and we experienced a disconnect. Heaven, to us, was a destination, not a resource. We knew nothing about learning to live from our spirits. We only knew what we had been doing all our lives since birth, and that was to live to satisfy our soul or our flesh. We sorely need to learn an alternative way of living.

Exchanging Our Way of Living

Paul recorded these words in his letter to the Romans:

> *Those who are motivated by the flesh only pursue what benefits themselves. But those who live by the impulses of the Holy Spirit are motivated to pursue spiritual realities. (Romans 8:5)*

We must learn to live spirit first! We must exchange our way of living. We must learn to live from our spirit. We need to understand the hierarchy within us:

a. We are a spirit.
b. We possess a soul.
c. We live in a body.

Each component has a specific purpose in our lives. Our spirit is the interface with the supernatural realm. It is designed for interfacing with Heaven and the Kingdom realm. Our spirit has been in existence in our body since conception. Our soul has a different purpose. It communicates to our intellect and our physical body what our spirit has obtained from Heaven. It is the interface with our body. Our body houses the two components and follows the dictates of whichever component is dominating,

Most of us have never been taught about having our spirit dominate. Rather, we have merely assumed that our soul being dominant was the required mode of operation.

Our soul always wants to be in charge. Our soul is susceptible to carnal or fleshly desires, lusts, and behaviors. It will, at times, resist our spirit and body. It must be made to submit to our spirit by an act of our will.

Our will is a means of instructing either component (spirit, soul, or body) in what to do. Our soul has a will, and so does our spirit. We choose who dominates!

Our body, on the other hand, has appetites that will control us in subjection to our soul. They become partners in crime—remember that second piece of chocolate cake it wanted? Our body will try, along with our soul, to dictate our behavior. It will likely resist the spirit's domination of our lives. However, it will obey our spirit's domination if instructed, and our body can aid our spirit if trained to do so.

The typical expression that operates in most people's lives is that their soul is first, body second, and their spirit is somewhere in the distance in last place.

In some people, especially those very conscious of their physical fitness or physical appearance, there is a different lineup. Their body is their priority, the soul second, and again, their spirit is the lowest priority.

Heaven's desire for us is vastly different. Heaven desires that we live spirit first, soul second, and body third. Since we are spiritual beings, this is the optimal arrangement. For most of us, our spirit was not activated in our lives in any measure until we became born again.

If, after our salvation experience, we began to pursue our relationship with the Father, then we became much more aware of our spirit and learned to live more spirit-conscious. The apostle Paul wrote in his various epistles about living in the spirit or walking in the spirit.

> *Because we are spiritual beings, our spirits cry out for a deepening of relationship with the Father.*

Our spirit longs for it and will try to steer us in that direction. Many of us had a hunger for God from early in our lives.

Our soul has certain characteristics that explain its behavior in our life. This is the briefest of lists, but I think we will get the idea. Our soul is selfish. It wants what it wants when it wants it. It can be very pouty. It can act like a small child. It is offendable and often even looks for opportunities to be offended. Our soul is also rude.

Our body has a different set of characteristics. It is inconsiderate, demanding, lazy, and self-serving. It does not want to get out of bed in the morning, for many people. In others, it wants to be fed things that are not beneficial.

However, the characteristics of our spirit are hugely different. If we live out of our spirit, we will find that we are loving and prone to be gentle. We desire peace. We are considerate. We are far more contented when living out of our spirit. Also, joy will often have a great expression in our lives.

Sometimes, we have experienced traumas that create a situation of our soul not trusting our spirit. The soul blames the spirit for not protecting it. The irony is that, typically, our soul never gave place to the spirit so that it could protect us. The soul places false blame on the spirit, and it must be coerced to forgive the spirit. Then, the soul must relinquish control to the spirit. Once the soul forgives the spirit, the two components can begin to work in harmony.

If I were to flash an image of some delicious, freshly cooked donuts in front of us, what would happen? For many, their body would announce a craving for one. What if, instead, I showed an image of a bowl of broccoli? How many people would get excited about that? Probably not as much excitement over a bowl of broccoli would be exhibited. Which does our body prefer—the donuts or broccoli? For the untamed soul, the donuts are likely to win out every time. Which do most kids prefer?

In any case, we can train ourselves to go for the healthier option. A principle regarding this that I heard years ago is summed up like this:

What we feed will live—
what we starve will die

What do we want to be dominant—our spirit, our soul, or our body? The part we feed is the part that will dominate.

For some, they feed their soul and live by the logic of their mind. Everything must be reasoned out in their mind before they will accept it. However, because our soul gains its insight from the Tree of the Knowledge of Good and Evil, it will always have faulty and limited understandings.

How do we change this soul-dominant or body-dominant pattern? We instruct our soul to back up and we call our spirit to come forward. Some people may need to physically stand up and speak to our soul and say, "Soul, back up," and as they say those words, take a physical step backward. Then, speak to their spirit out loud and say, "Spirit, come forward." As we speak those words, take a physical step forward. This prophetic act helps trigger a shift within them.

Live spirit first!

Benefits of Living Spirit First

Why would we want to live spirit first? Let me present several reasons. Living spirit first will create in us an increased awareness of Heaven and the realms of Heaven. It will create a deeper comprehension of the presence of Holy Spirit, of angels, and men and women in white linen. We will be able to better hear the voice of Heaven. We will experience greater creativity, productivity, hope, and peace. We will become more aware of the needs of people that we meet.

As we live spirit first, we will be able to access the riches of Heaven in our life. Petty things that formerly bothered us will dissipate in importance or impact in our lives. We will be able to move ahead, not concerned with the petty, mundane, or unproductive things that have affected our lives before we begin to live spirit first.

This way of life is more than a game changer—for the believer, it is the only way to live. We will face challenges as we build our business or live our life from Heaven down, but we will more readily be able to access the solutions of Heaven as we live with an awareness of the richness of Heaven and all that is available to us as a son or daughter of the Lord Most High. Do not live dominated by the soul. *Live **spirit first!***

———— ∞ ————

Resources from LifeSpring International Ministries

A visit to the **RonHorner.com** website will give a glimpse of the various branches of ministry we are involved in. We started providing coaching to people within the Courts of Heaven, advocating for them and their situations. Our corporate name is LifeSpring International Ministries, Inc., a North Carolina registered nonprofit corporation.

Personal Advocacy Sessions

Known as Personal Advocacy Sessions, these 90-minute sessions with our trained team of advocates have successfully worked with a myriad of situations. If you have an issue that you can't seem to get breakthrough about, schedule a session with our advocates.

LifeSpring Mentoring Group

Since starting this weekly class on Zoom in 2019, we have taught on the Courts of Heaven, protocols, engaging Heaven for revelation, working with angels and men and women white linen, lingering human spirits, and more. It is a free class. Simply visit **ronhorner.com** to register for the link for the class.

Membership Program

We have several tiers of membership for those tracking with us. The Platinum level gains you access to our library of videos, blogs, and more.

LifeSpring School of Ministry

A trimester-based school to help you grow in your walk. Trimester 1 focuses on cleansing your generations. Trimester 2 focuses on Protocols of the Courts of Heaven, and Trimester 3 focuses on Advanced Protocols of the Courts of Heaven. Completion of Trimesters 1, 2, and 3 will qualify the student for consideration as a Junior or Senior Advocate able to conduct Personal Advocacy Sessions with our clients.

CourtsNet

CourtsNet is our video-based training program offering a wide variety of classes and courses. Some are free.

AfterCare

Not every situation is solved by the Courts of Heaven. Sometimes, people need to learn simple things to navigate life. Our AfterCare program provides Biblical counseling (not Courts of Heaven focused), classes, and groups regularly.

Sandhills Ecclesia

In 2022, we started a Sunday Gathering known as Sandhills Ecclesia (that's the name we saw on the book in Heaven when we went to inquire.) My wife, Adina, and I live in the area of North Carolina known as the Sandhills region, thus the name. We meet weekly at 11:00 AM Eastern, and on the first Sunday of the month, we have an afternoon gathering to do legislative work in the Courts of Heaven as a group. All are welcome. Simply visit **sandhillsecclesia.com** and register for the link.

Heaven Down Business

Heaven Down Business is a worldwide coaching and consultancy business designed to assist entrepreneurs and business owners in implementing the Heaven Down™ Business Building paradigm into their business. For more information, visit **heavendownbusiness.com**.

Adina's Melodies/Heaven Down Music

Adina Horner, co-founder of LifeSpring, is a gifted minstrel and has several albums of prophetic worship music available on several of the most popular music platforms. Visit **adinasmelodies.com**.

LifeSpring Publishing/Scroll Publishers

LifeSpring Publishing primarily publishes Dr. Ron's books, and Scroll Publishers is our imprint where we publish the books of others relating to engaging Heaven, living spirit forward, and the Heaven Down™ lifestyle.

YouTube Channel

Our most recent videos from the Mentoring Group are posted on YouTube®. Visit our YouTube® channel,

courtsofheavenwebinar on YouTube® for the latest videos.

Visit our website:

RonHorner.com

Our website, **RonHorner.com,** has a myriad of resources, many of which are free, as well as numerous videos.

———— ∞ ————

Works Cited

(2025, February 22). Retrieved from Merriam-Webster.com Dictionary: https://www.merriam-webster.com/dictionary/have%20a%20chip%20on%20one%27s%20shoulder

Rubies. (2025, February 18). Retrieved from Google.com: https://www.google.com/search?client=firefox-b-1-d&q=rubies

What does bride mean in the Bible? (2025, February 18). Retrieved from Bible Dictionary Today: www.bibledictionarytoday.com/words/bride

Description

Embracing Your Crown of Authority is a transformative guide to understanding and stepping into your God-given authority. Many believers live beneath their divine potential, unaware of the spiritual crowns they are meant to wear. This book unveils the power, responsibility, and divine inheritance that come with each crown, equipping you to walk in greater confidence, wisdom, and kingdom influence.

Through biblical insights, revelatory teachings, and practical applications, *Embracing Your Crown of Authority* will help you:

- Recognize the crowns bestowed upon you by God.
- Understand their significance and how to activate them in your life.
- Overcome spiritual opposition that seeks to rob you of your authority.

- Walk in greater alignment with your divine purpose.

Whether you are seeking deeper spiritual growth, clarity in your calling, or empowerment to navigate life's challenges with divine authority, this book offers a roadmap to fully embrace your spiritual identity. It's time to rise, wear your crowns, and reign in the fullness of your God-given destiny.

──── ∞ ────

About the Author

Dr. Ron Horner is an apostolic teacher specializing in the Courts of Heaven and divine revelation. He has written nearly forty books on the Courts of Heaven, engaging Heaven, working with angels, or living from revelation.

He currently trains people to engage with the Courts of Heaven in a weekly online teaching session. You can register to participate and discover more about the Courts of Heaven prayer paradigm on his various websites, classes, products, and services found here:

www.ronhorner.com

——— ∞ ———

Other Books by Dr. Ron M. Horner

Building Your Business from Heaven Down

Building Your Business from Heaven Down 2.0

Building Your Business with the Blueprint of Heaven

Commissioning Angels – Volume 1

Cooperating with the Glory

Courts of Heaven Process Charts

Dealing with Trusts & Consequential Liens

Embracing Your Crown of Authority

Embracing Crowns for Governmental Intercession

Embracing Crowns for Your Business

Embracing Crowns for Your Family

Engaging Angels in the Realms of Heaven

Engaging Heaven for Revelation – Volume 1

Engaging Heaven for Revelation – Volume 2

Engaging Heaven for Trade

Engaging the Courts for Ownership & Order

Engaging the Courts for Your City (*Paperback, Leader's Guide & Workbook*)

Engaging the Courts of Healing & the Healing Garden

Engaging the Courts of Heaven

Engaging the Help Desk of the Courts of Heaven

Four Keys to Dismantling Accusations

Freedom from Mithraism

Kingdom Dynamics – Volume 1

Kingdom Dynamics – Volume 2

Let's Get it Right!

Lingering Human Spirits

Lingering Human Spirits – Volume 2

Living Spirit Forward

Maximizing Your Crown of Authority

Next Dimension Access to the Court of Supplications

Overcoming the False Verdicts of Freemasonry

Overcoming Verdicts from the Courts of Hell

Releasing Bonds from the Courts of Heaven

The Courts of Heaven: An Introduction (formerly *Engaging the Mercy Court of Heaven*)

Unlocking Spiritual Seeing

Working with Your Realms and Your Realm Angels

SPANISH

Cómo Anular los Falsos Veredictos de la Masonería

Cómo Proceder en la Corte Celestial de Misericordia

Cómo Proceder en las Cortes para su Ciudad

Cómo Trabajar con Angeles en los Ambitos del Cielo

Cooperando con La Gloria de Dios

Las Cuatro Llaves para Anular las Acusaciones

Liberando Bonos en las Cortes Celestiales

Liberando Su Visión Espiritual

Sea Libre del Mitraísmo

Tablas de Proceso de la Cortes del Cielo

───── ∞ ─────

www.ingramcontent.com/pod-product-compliance
Lightning Source LLC
Chambersburg PA
CBHW021133230426
43667CB00005B/97